What's Worth Fighting For Out There?

ANDY HARGREAVES
AND
MICHAEL FULLAN

What's Worth Fighting For Out There?

Ontario Public School Teachers' Federation   An Affiliate of the Ontario Teachers' Federation

WHAT'S WORTH FIGHTING FOR OUT THERE?

Andy Hargreaves and Michael Fullan

Commissioned and published by
Ontario Public School Teachers' Federation
An Affiliate of the Ontario Teachers' Federation
5160 Orbitor Drive
Mississauga, Ontario, Canada L4W 5H2

As a commissioned publication, the ideas and examples cited in
What's Worth Fighting For Out There? are those of the authors
and do not necessarily represent the policies or positions of the
Ontario Public School Teachers' Federation.

ISBN 0-9680 759-4-0

Additional copies of this publication may be ordered by duplicating and
completing the order form inside the back cover.

 Printed in Canada

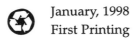 January, 1998
First Printing

FROM THE PRESIDENT

The Ontario Public School Teachers' Federation (OPSTF) published the first book in the **What's Worth Fighting For?** series in 1988. In ten Years *What's Worth Fighting For in the Principalship* and *What's Worth Fighting For? Working Together For Your School* have found their way into the mainstream of educational thinking around the globe.

As the authors and the OPSTF discussed the concept for the trilogy in the early stages of development, who could have ever predicted so accurately the timeliness of *What's Worth Fighting For Out There?* Examining the role of teachers and the function of schools in our society have never been more critical. Hargreaves and Fullan conclude that the relationship between those in the school and those outside it must be fundamentally reframed. To do this, they suggest we must go "wider" by developing new relationships and "deeper" into the heart of our practice.

The authors remind us that teaching is a passionate vocation. They identify hope as the ultimate virtue on which a decent and successful school system depends. Never has the challenge for teachers to remain passionate and hopeful been greater. Fortunately, as the authors write, "hope does not travel alone". *What's Worth Fighting For Out There?* explores ways that teachers, principals, parents, governments, businesses and others can work together to seek a way forward. The future of our society depends on concerted action by all constituencies.

As President of the Ontario Public School Teachers' Federation, I should like to express the appreciation of the OPSTF to Andy Hargreaves and Michael Fullan for the on-going contribution they make to our profession. *What's Worth Fighting For Out There?* gives us hope.

Phyllis Benedict
President, OPSTF

ACKNOWLEDGMENTS

We would like to thank the Ontario Public School Teachers' Federation for giving us the title 'What's Worth Fighting For', Linda Grant for her active support and recommendations throughout the project, and Joan Saunderson, Dean Fink, Mary Stager and Nancy Watson for very helpful comments. Leo Santos and Claudia Cuttress typed and produced the manuscript through many stages and we thank them both for their great commitment and effectiveness in bringing the book to a successful completion under very tight deadlines.

CONTENTS

FOREWORD

These days much is at stake for public education – and for the notion and reality of democracy. As access to knowledge increasingly divides the "haves" from the "have nots," societies are questioning whether and how they can enable all of their citizens to function in an increasingly complex world. Public schools are being asked to educate the most pluralistic group of students in history for more challenging learning than ever before. Teachers and other school leaders are expected to learn to teach in much more sophisticated ways that reach students who approach learning from diverse vantage points while restructuring schools designed many decades ago for a much different mission in a much simpler time.

To do all of this, educators must enlist parents, policy makers, and the public in support of the fundamental goals of public education and in support of fundamental change. This is no simple matter. There are the familiars of schooling that make change frightening, the matters of turf and privilege that threaten narrowly conceived self-interests, and the steep learning curves that accompany any new practice. *What's Worth Fighting For Out There?* confronts this daunting agenda with candor and realism but also with optimism that the fight can be won. School people will find it a welcome companion on the path to progressive reform. Hopefully, parents, policy makers, and committed members of the public will learn that they can contribute from this fresh and engaging look at what it will take to build a new system that succeeds with today's students for tomorrow's demands.

It has recently become fashionable to note the importance of community by quoting the old African proverb, "It takes a whole village to raise a child." *What's Worth Fighting For Out There?* takes this important concept a step further by asking "What does it take to raise a village?" The answer, thoughtfully woven within these pages, is well worth reading because we learn how to raise 'the whole village' in the service of deep educational reform.

Linda Darling-Hammond
William F. Russell Professor in Education, Teachers College, Columbia University

PREFACE

The future of teaching is in the hands of those who turn hope into an active virtue.

Our **What's Worth Fighting For** trilogy is designed to help teachers and principals "fight for" fundamentally positive changes that will benefit themselves, students and society, and to do this with the full knowledge of the reality of the task. Our goal in this series is to achieve deeper analysis that can generate more powerful action. In the face of complexity, insight and practicality must go hand in hand.

The first in the trilogy, *What's Worth Fighting For in the Principalship?* was primarily addressing school administrators. The "Principalship" book has now been revised and updated in a second edition (Fullan, 1997). The argument is that principals are increasingly overloaded and that the "system" fosters dependency. The most productive response to this perverse state of affairs lies in seeking deeper insights and corresponding action guidelines which are more accessible to leaders themselves. *What's Worth Fighting For in the Principalship?* sets the stage for all leaders – principals, teachers and others – to take more control despite the system.

In the second book – *What's Worth Fighting For? Working Together for Your School* we examine the culture of the school, starting with the observation that schools are not now learning organizations either for students or for teachers. We discuss four types of school cultures - fragmented individualism, balkanization, contrived collegiality, and collaboration. Only the latter has potential for continuous learning. We provide ideas for principals and teachers to change the current situation. Eight guidelines for principals and twelve for teachers lay out some of the core starting points and most powerful levers for change.

The present book is the final entry in the trilogy. In *What's Worth Fighting For Out There?* we conclude that the relationship between those in the school and those outside it must be fundamentally reframed. In a world of growing complexity and rapid change, if we are going to bring about significant improvements in teaching and learning *within* schools, we must forge strong, open, and interactive connections with communities *beyond* them. To do this we must go "wider" by developing new relationships with parents, employers, universities, technology, and the broader profession. We must also go "deeper" into the heart of our practice by rediscovering the passion and moral purpose that makes teaching and learning exciting and effective. The closing "Guidelines for Action" for principals, teachers, governments and parents in *What's Worth Fighting For Out There?* show just what it means to go wider and deeper in this way.

Chapter 1 focusses on 'what's' out there; Chapters 2 and 3 on 'why' we must go deeper and wider, and Chapter 4 on 'how' to get out there. In Chapter 1 we talk about 'what's out there' and what it means for principals and teachers. In a word, it is frightening. Never before have teachers been so vulnerable and so important at the same time. Never before have the boundaries between the school and its environment become so permeable and transparent. What's "out there" and what's 'in here' become more and more difficult to distinguish.

In Chapter 2 we propose that part of the answer means *going deeper,* reaching down in to the moral purpose, emotion and hope that is at the heart of good teaching. Going deeper on one's own is a recipe for burnout and moral martyrdom. The deeper you go into teaching the more help you realize you need. Teachers can only be effective in large numbers when they also *go wider*. We describe in Chapter 3 what it means to go wider in working differently with parents and the community, governments, technology, business and the wider profession.

The closing chapter develops "Guidelines for Action" for getting there. These guidelines are written for teachers and principals to help them go deeper and wider in their thinking and practice, and to show policy makers and communities what they can do and why they should do it for the sake of the future of children and society. As the entire trilogy argues, the difficulty is that, under conditions of fragmentation and diversity, we must develop relationships in many instances with people we do not understand, or even trust. Our action guidelines contain ideas for how we might go about this difficult business.

The writing style in the *What's Worth Fighting For* series is intended to make accessible ideas steeped in theory, research and practice. Our goal in the series is to expand the boundaries and depth of analysis with insights and action guidelines that are both accessible and inspiring. We want to provoke thought, elicit debate and encourage action.

Teaching has always been an emotional profession. The difference nowadays is that it is transparently emotional, open for all to see and criticize. In the short run, this new visibility can be destructive. In the long run, we believe that it is both inevitable and desirable because it holds open the promise of mobilizing resources, without which the job of teaching can no longer be done. In *What's Worth Fighting For? Working Together for Your School* we said that the walls of the classroom are and should 'crumble', metaphorically speaking. In *What's Worth Fighting For Out There?* we say that the walls of the school are and should come tumbling down.

To get out there is going to require hopefulness and assertiveness when despair and defeatism can easily be justified. We will show that going deeper means having hope, even when the conditions do not seem to warrant it. The future of the teaching profession is in the hands of those who turn hope into an active virtue.

Chapter 1
WHAT'S OUT THERE

"Teaching is the most inherently hopeful act that I know of."

Patricia Murphy (Teacher, Ottawa)
Toronto Globe and Mail, September 11, 1996

Introduction

Patricia Murphy teaches a group of special education children. Such children, she says are often labelled "emotionally disturbed, difficult, violent and unteachable." Her experience is different. She gets "to share in the progress and achievements of a group of children who know that the odds are against them, but learn anyway." In Patricia Murphy's eyes, teaching is inherently hopeful because. . .

> You've got it within you to succeed in life, to be happy and to be proud of yourself. No matter what anyone has told you, no matter what you believe right now, you've got it.

When an individual teacher believes this, she can improve a life. When large numbers of teachers can come to believe it, they can do a whole world of good. There is systematic evidence that teachers who have a strong sense of their own *efficacy*, who believe they can make a real difference in their students' lives, really do (Ashton & Webb, 1986). The prophecy is self-fulfilling. And it works in even the most challenging communities. Hope, optimism and self-belief among teachers are the vital wellsprings of successful learning and positive educational change. Without them, classrooms are likely to become barren wastelands of boredom and routine, and schools will turn into deserts of lost opportunity.

It is individuals who must hope, but it is institutions that create the climate and conditions which make people feel more hopeful – or less so. We know that schools work like this because schools where teachers' senses of efficacy or self-belief are weakest are also ones where teachers work in isolation, lack support and recognition, and experience feelings of powerlessness and alienation. Just to urge teachers to look on the bright side and be more hopeful is not enough. The insensitivities of many imposed reforms, the indignities inflicted by political and media criticism, and change efforts which turn over so rapidly that they can't be implemented properly are draining the optimism of teachers.

Teachers all over the world are feeling beleaguered. Teachers in England express their reactions to impending high-stakes inspection of their school, and to the detailed paper accountability which this demands.

> *Whatever criticism they make, it's going to feel, however stupid it is, that the last 20 years have been for nothing. It's not about what progress schools have made in the last 15 years. It's "Schools fail." "Head (principal) to be removed." "Hit team going in." It doesn't matter what you look at. It's about failure in schools.*

> *I don't want to lose my optimism. People always say I am optimistic but I am beginning to lose it. I don't want to be negative, for I enjoy some parts, but I'm worrying about the level of support for others I can sustain (as a teacher leader) as I see them suffering more and more . . . We seem to have become (whiners) but that is not really who we are.*

> (Jeffrey & Woods, 1997)

Australian primary teachers respond to far-reaching reforms in the state of Victoria.

> *They don't really care, it's purely a numbers and monetary game.*

> *They treat us like imbeciles and incorrectly view us as a politically aware and radical group, as "opposition." They have a low opinion of us and we are being punished – pulled into line and disempowered.*

Where's it all leading to? . . . you get to the point where you say, does it matter? I've cut back here because of the way I've been treated.

(they treat us as) bodies to be burnt out . . . In the last five years, a lot of joy went out of teaching.

(Bishop and Mulford, 1996)

A Canadian teacher we interviewed in a study of Grade 7 and 8 teachers reflects that:

You know (the media say) we whine . . . , we make too much money and people take this really, really seriously. And I guess I've never been on the receiving end of teacher bashing . . . I mean people who know me, know how many hours I put in, and how committed to the job I am, and what I do for the kids, and when I tell them that I find clothes for this kid, and I drive this kid home, they just go – "what?"! . . . it gets people down reading this stuff over and over and over again . . . Then the board is going through this whole renewal thing. Then we are working without a contract this year, and there is talk of a strike . . . I think it just wears people down . . . But I think there is that . . . constant sort of taking a sore and keeping rubbing away at it, until it gets a little worse and a little more infected and then you've got attitude. And I think as the kids present attitude and we're getting attitude then we tend to give attitude. It's just . . . not a very nice time to be a teacher.

Even passionate teachers, says Fried (1995), are exhausted in the face of apathy and resistance from those around them. Too much educational reform and restructuring is destroying teachers' confidence, draining their energy, eating up their time and taking away their hope.

The *Times Education Supplement* (1997, April) in a survey of 1000 teachers in England calls it "the feel-bad factor":

Morale in Britain's staff rooms has hit rock bottom. Teachers are feeling disillusioned, demoralized and angry at being forced to carry out unpopular government policies while being constantly blamed for society's ills.

3

What's Worth Fighting For Out There? makes two equal claims. It tells "society" that until it realizes that the quality and morale of teachers is absolutely central to the well-being of students and their learning, all serious reform efforts are bound to fail. Second, it says that teachers cannot wait for society to get it right. They will become their own worst enemies if they do not take action to help break the current deadlock of despair that envelopes public school systems everywhere.

In *What's Worth Fighting For? Working Together for Your School* we stressed that teachers and principals could combat what they experience as negative trends by bonding together in collaborative work cultures. How teachers work with each other, we showed, affects how well they work with their students. Pursuing continuous improvement together makes more sense than complying with changes from outside, or rejecting change altogether. Moreover, cultures of collaboration strengthen teachers' sense of common purpose and enable them to interact assertively with external pressures for change – adopting changes that they value, selectively incorporating aspects of them that fit their own purposes, and rejecting ones that are seen as educationally unsound or irrelevant.

But even professional collaboration is no longer sufficient. Teachers who work with other teachers are sometimes less inclined to work with anyone else. Collaboration can include the school professionals but exclude the wider community. And when families, communities and workplaces are changing as rapidly and dramatically as they are today, this flaw can be fatal. In times of turbulent social change, redefining one's relationship to the environment is crucial. What sort of curriculum should teachers teach in increasingly diverse classrooms? Who will help them cope with the consequences of increased child poverty that absorb their time and have little to do with teaching at all? How should they respond to the constant criticisms and demands for results that are endlessly hurled at them? The environment around schools is not only more complex and volatile. It is also increasingly part and parcel of our everyday existence. What's "out there" is now 'in here', and this calls for radically different strategies and conditions for learning, improving and simply surviving in schools today.

We believe it is necessary to broaden our approach to educational change and school improvement. We also know that our case is not an easy one to argue. Many teachers are already overwhelmed by pressures for change *within* their own schools and classrooms. Don't they have enough to deal with already, without having to attend to yet more demands – demands that will now require teachers to extend their work beyond the school into homes, communities and workplaces? Aren't we in danger of making schools into dumping grounds for social and economic problems that are really other people's responsibility? Are teachers to be at the beck and call of every pushy parent and pressure group that has a bee in its bonnet or an axe to grind? Surely the last thing we need is yet more diversion of teachers' effort and energies away from working with students in their own classrooms!

We sympathize with these objections and reservations. It is true that many specious changes have been brought about under the banner of creating better partnerships between schools and other organizations. There are times when partnerships with industry have led to corporate dollars driving the curriculum in dubious directions; when partnerships with faculties of education have come down to teachers in schools carrying the faculty's staff supervision load for them; and when partnerships with parents have amounted to little more than cosmetic committee work, or to appeasing the demands of an aggressive minority. It is also true that teachers have become increasingly and unreasonably buffeted by the single-issue demands of various interest groups, and by the capricious policy whims of successive governments. Partnerships are not always benevolent and pressure groups outside the school frequently have more than the children's interests at heart.

So why should teachers and principals work with others outside the school for better teaching and learning within it when so many outside demands are politically suspect or bureaucratically time-consuming? What's the problem here?

What Are The Problems?

Our argument in a nutshell is best expressed by de Gues in *The Living Company* (1997):

> *to cope with a changing world, any entity must develop the capability of shifting and changing, of developing new skills and attitudes: in short the capability of learning . . . the essence of learning is the ability to manage change by changing yourself – as much for people when they grow up as for companies when they live through turmoil (p. 20).*

To gain greater control over the environment we must change our stance towards it. There are several reasons why schools need to connect more effectively with the wider world beyond them:

1. schools cannot shut their gates and leave the outside world on the doorstep;

2. more diversity demands greater flexibility;

3. the technology juggernaut is breaking down the walls of schooling;

4. schools are one of our last hopes for rescuing and reinventing community;

5. teachers can do with more help; and so can parents and communities;

6. education is essential for democracy;

7. market competition, parental choice and individual self-management are redefining how schools relate to their wider environments;

8. schools can no longer be indifferent to what kinds of living and working await their students when they move into the adult world;

9. the pressures of today's complex environments are relentless, and contradictory; *and*

10. our existing structures are exhausted.

1. SCHOOLS CANNOT SHUT THEIR GATES AND LEAVE THE OUTSIDE WORLD ON THE DOORSTEP.

> *For teachers, what's "out there" beyond their school is not an academic abstraction or a futuristic projection.*

Schools can no longer pretend that their walls will keep the outside world at bay. As Elkind (1997) says, they have become porous and permeable institutions. Increased poverty creates hungry children who cannot learn and tired ones who cannot concentrate. Fractured, blended and lone parent families fill teachers' classes with children who are often troubled, presenting teachers with parents' nights of labyrinthine complexity; also leaving teachers with outdated curriculum materials where families with two parents and their own biological children are presented as the cultural norm. Increased rates and changing patterns of global migration coupled with continuing low levels of teacher recruitment from visible minorities, mean that teachers are often teaching "other people's children" whose backgrounds are unfamiliar to them and whose learning needs are unknown (Delpit, 1993). In some of the large urban school districts with which we have worked, over 50% of the students are classified as English as a Second Language and over 70 languages are spoken in the schools. For teachers, what's "out there" beyond their school is not an academic abstraction or a futuristic projection. It stares back at them everyday through the eyes of the students they teach. The issue is not whether teachers connect with what's "out there" beyond their school, but how effectively they do so.

2. MORE DIVERSITY DEMANDS GREATER FLEXIBILITY.

A culturally diverse student population should not mean business-as-usual in our classrooms, with a few adjustments for cultural and language differences added on. The changes that are needed extend beyond recognizing a few more cultural festivals or adding specific components of second language learning. They reach right down to the basic principles of teaching and learning itself.

Not only are many classes highly heterogeneous in terms of ethnicity, cultural meaning, recency of immigration, etc., but there is also so much else going on in the outside lives of students. In the homogeneous classrooms of yesterday a strict well prepared teacher could at least reach those interested in learning. Not so today. It has always been the case that teaching means reaching the student. It is just so much more difficult to do it these days.

Dryden (1995) noted that: "so much is going on in each kid's life, every story is so complicated" (p. 84). Students are often disengaged from their own learning, and it is enormously difficult for teachers to enter their world.

Given the cultural mix of students, there are few common contents taught to the class as a whole, that would conceivably engage all students. Factor in special education students who have increasingly been integrated into regular classes, and the diversity is greater still. Diversity demands flexibility. Properly accommodating diversities in culture, language and learning styles means fundamentally rethinking the very core of what we teach and how we teach it. For teachers everywhere, this is a daunting and inescapable challenge.

3. THE TECHNOLOGY JUGGERNAUT IS BREAKING DOWN THE WALLS OF SCHOOLING.

Schooling is now available in cyberspace.

Around 40% of young people in North America now have access to a personal computer at home. Many more make extensive use of television, video and the music culture of the streets. For the youth of today, the geography of learning stretches far beyond the physical space of the school. New technologies enable many students to reach out and connect with other students, other teachers, other worlds: to surf the internet and ride the information superhighway without the teacher's immediate monitoring,

8

support and intervention. Learning can often take place as easily at home as at school. Schooling is now available in cyberspace. Indeed, home-schooling is enjoying a significant rise in popularity. Students often know more about technology than their teachers and are able to access learning more easily through it. Unless teachers get up to speed in using technology in their classrooms, the hold they have on their students will weaken. Moreover, as we shall argue in Chapter 3, unless teachers become experts in *designing pedagogy* for using technology, computers will do more harm than good.

In their rush to compete with the computer age, and to keep their children's attention, teachers run the risk of reducing education to entertainment and losing sight of their larger purposes as a result (Postman, 1992; Stoll, 1995). The computer age is chipping away at the walls of schooling and at the autonomy and authority of teachers within them. By permitting worldwide communication at the tap of a keyboard, computer technology dissolves the distinction between what's "out there" and what's "in here" altogether. Teachers should not capitulate unthinkingly to new technology but they clearly cannot turn away from it either. Their students and the society in which we live will not let them.

Like all of the forces we talk about, globalization and technology can be destructive and liberating depending on how we relate to them. We have no choice in deciding whether technology will affect us. The only choice is figuring out how we will change ourselves and each other to respond to it and turn it to our advantage.

4. SCHOOLS ARE ONE OF OUR LAST HOPES FOR RESCUING AND REINVENTING COMMUNITY.

> *A good school is the price of peace in the community.*
> Ursula Franklin (1997)

Science and technology, rational planning and modernization have eroded tradition and eliminated the places where community once thrived. The friendly clutter of the corner store has been replaced by the sleek lines and anonymity of the pedestrian precinct and the shopping mall. Many members of the middle class have deserted the city for the safety of the suburbs where neighbours often care more for their lawns than they do for each other. In many communities, affiliation with major Christian churches is in decline, as is attendance at religious services. Only on the television programme "Cheers", it seems, can most people find a place where "everybody knows your name." The price of consumer affluence has been anonymity and alienation. And the heaviest price has been paid by those too poor to participate in the consumer society at all, eking out their existence in the dislocation and desolation of the old inner cities which modernization has left behind.

Recently, there are signs that people are struggling to recreate a sense of community, and the meaning and support that are to be found there. As Reid (1996:29) reports in a survey of Canadians: "In a world in which the permanence of just about every other relationship can't be taken for granted, family and friends seem to matter more than ever."

Because of its geographical convenience and its connection to the lives of many families, the neighbourhood school is the most obvious focus for community building efforts. As Ursula Franklin (1997) has enigmatically put it: "a good school is the price of peace in the community".

5.   TEACHERS CAN DO WITH MORE HELP; AND SO CAN PARENTS AND COMMUNITIES.

The point about community is not just that schools can serve their wider communities better, but that these communities can also be an active source of support for teachers in school. And teachers can certainly do with the help. More and more social work and paperwork are getting in the way of classroom work with children. Scarcely a week goes by without schools being confronted by more imposition of endless change. Above all, teachers need support because education should be viewed as a shared responsibility among many parts of society.

In *What's Worth Fighting For? Working Together for Your School* we showed how working more closely with colleagues could reduce duplication, share the burden, provide moral support and give teachers the collective strength to set priorities among all the demands that are placed upon them. But even this is no longer enough. The pressure for teachers to change their classroom practice towards more intensive work with individuals and small groups so as to accommodate the multiple intelligences and varied learning styles of culturally diverse students, means that teachers need help inside the classroom as well as collegial support outside it. This means bringing the community into the school and the classroom to offer clerical support, help in preparing materials, supervision of needy students, and assistance with children's reading. All these kinds of support already have a strong record of success in many schools although, as we shall show later, they need to be extended and developed further. Where school-community relations are concerned we have barely begun to scratch the surface.

To say that teachers need more help is not to imply they are somewhat incapable, inadequate or cannot cope. Giving and asking for help works best when it is reciprocal, when teaching is seen as inherently difficult – as something that everyone needs help with; not just those who are weak, or new to the job. The same applies to the help teachers need from parents or other members of the community. To want this help is not to be professionally wanting – but to recognize that doing the increasingly difficult and complex work of teaching means harnessing all the human resources you can get. As our late colleague Matt Miles put it: "seeking help is a sign of intelligence not weakness." Indeed, there is a good deal of evidence that the more successful a school is and the more it reaches out to engage more and more partners, then the stronger it becomes.

Similarly, teachers who act as if they have something to learn as well as something to contribute, establish better learning relationships with students and parents. Many teachers will have to learn to use their specialized expertise not to separate themselves from parents, and other adults, but to redefine their relationships with other adults in ways that allow them to be both open *and* authoritative. Patients prefer medical general practitioners who are properly qualified, know their stuff and keep up-to-date. They also like GPs who give them time, listen properly to how they describe their ailments, explain their diagnosis and treatments clearly, and are open and honest when they don't know what the diagnosis is. So should it be with teachers and other adults – teachers should be confident in their expertise, clear and reciprocal in their communication, and not pretend to be perfect or infallible about the judgements they make. Becoming more open and authoritative as professionals is one of the things that is truly worth fighting for to improve teachers' relations with other adults in their schools and wider communities.

The flip side of teachers needing help is that parents and communities need it too. It is time to stop demonizing teachers while idealizing parents and communities. As Steinberg (1996) observes:

> The first, and most significant, problem is the high prevalence of disengaged parents in contemporary America. By our estimate, nearly one in three parents in America is seriously disengaged from his or her adolescent's life, and especially from the adolescent's education (1996: 187).

For at least a decade we have known that efforts to engage parents and communities with teachers can reap enormous dividends for students' learning, especially those from disadvantaged circumstances (Epstein, 1995). There is no reason to believe that parents are automatically better at their role than teachers. Both need to develop new skills and attitudes to raise young people better in a rapidly changing world.

Most schools now connect poorly with their communities. Too many are not even good communities in themselves. This is especially true of large, specialized high schools. The bigger schools get, the more impersonal they become; the more exclusively academic is their focus, the less they are able to care for their clients (be they students or parents). Some critics have likened secondary schools to overcrowded airports where students have to rush between lessons like dashing between flights, and where they have little or no space, no place to belong of their own (D. Hargreaves, 1982).

In turning schools into stronger communities, school reforms should not be separated from wider urban reform. They depend on each other. Many of the problems that plague urban schools stem from the problems of cities themselves. The full solution lies outside the schools as well as within them. This is not an excuse for schools to sit back and wait for the city to change. It is a rallying cry for the two to work together more closely. However, that doesn't mean that you have to work on all issues at once. Rather, as Walsh (1997) says: "the best projects tackle what they are best positioned to make a difference on and work out from there" (p. 36). Teachers and parents need each other and need to learn from each other in order to do the job of teaching and learning better.

6. EDUCATION IS ESSENTIAL FOR DEMOCRACY.

Family is not always the best metaphor for community.

Communities are not always democracies. Small town nostalgia is not the sense of community we are advocating here – where community is inward-looking and ethnically homogeneous. Communities today must look outward as well as inward and must include and give voice to all their members. Some advocates of community restoration present rather paternalistic notions of community where duty, loyalty and service are paramount. Here community goes with hierarchy. In many schools that describe themselves as families, the managerial professionals effectively become the school while everyone else is treated like dependent children. Family is not always the best metaphor for community.

Like others, we believe that schools should build not just any kind of community, but *democratic communities* which value participation, equality, inclusiveness and social justice, in addition to loyalty and service among all their members (Merz & Fuhrman, 1997). These communities should start in the classrooms in which students share responsibility for their own learning and for regulating each others' behaviour. Involving students and parents in decision-making, teaching and learning decisions, parent conferences and assessment of achievement extend these democratic principles further. Public education has an important role to play in developing and maintaining democratic societies. Goodlad (1997) begins his chapter on 'Education and Democracy' with these words:

There is a contextual surround that invariably shapes the educational process. The political context is critical. The shaping that takes place in a fascist or communist regime is quite different from that in a democracy. The social context is equally, or perhaps even more critical. People who live by sword or gun raise their children by very different beliefs than do people who value negotiation as the proper way to resolve disagreements (p. 23).

He continues: "what we have in mind . . . is education that develops in humans the dispositions to make choices that benefit self and community mutually" (p. 43).

Democracy, in many nations that take pride in the word, is in jeopardy. This is not because the military runs the government or elections have come to an end, but because more and more people are withdrawing from political participation and public life. In *The Culture of Contentment*, Galbraith (1992) describes how people have become increasingly disillusioned with politics and politicians. They vote less, care less, trust less. People mourn for religious and cultural leaders now, not for political figures. The comfortably-off, says Galbraith, have withdrawn into a culture of self-absorbed contentment. Meanwhile, the poor and the marginalized have sunk into alienation and despair. Politics is in peril, public commitment is in decline and democracy is in danger of becoming a shell of what it should be.

Historian, David Labaree (1997) says that for many decades, American education has been treated as a private good not a public good. It has put individual competitive achievement before civic duty and improving the quality of public life for all. All the democratic ideals of citizenship, equity and thoughtful choice to which John Dewey and other leading thinkers committed themselves for so long have been overwhelmed by test scores, content coverage and competitive achievement in an educational war of all against all. If the democracy of public life is endangered now, it is in part because we are now having to reap socially what we have sown educationally in the past.

Can we maintain a healthy democracy in the absence of a healthy *public* school system? We and others think not.

In Galbraith's (1996:17) 'Good Society':

> *Education not only makes democracy possible; it also makes it essential.*
> *Education not only brings into existence a population with an*
> *understanding of the public tasks; it also creates their demand to be*
> *heard."*

Similarly Saul (1995) says that the primary purpose of education is "to show individuals how they can function *together* in a society" (p. 138.) And further,

> *[Democracy] continues to exist only through the daily efforts of its*
> *citizenry [who must] delight in the human condition of sympathy of*
> *others versus self-loathing and cynicism regarding the qualities of*
> *others (p. 155).*

In modern societies the relationship between democracy and schooling has always been too abstract, or perhaps taken for granted and thereby often neglected. It should no longer be. Teachers and parents observe democracy deteriorating every time the gap between a privileged and unprivileged learner widens, every time the public school system weakens and independent schools become the institutions of choice for those who can afford it.

As Saul concludes:

> *The existence of high quality national public education school systems*
> *for the first dozen or so years of training is the key to democracy where*
> *legitimacy lies with the citizen. At first hearing, this may sound like a*
> *motherhood statement. But the reality is that throughout the West –*
> *not just in the United States – we are slipping away from that simple*
> *principle of high quality public education. And, in doing so, we are*
> *further undermining democracy (p. 65).*

Public schools need to develop more of what Coleman (1990) termed 'social capital' or what we call civic community – to help produce citizens who have the commitment, skills and dispositions to foster norms of civility, compassion, fairness, justice, sharing, trust, collaborative engagement, and constructive critiques in conditions of great social diversity.

15

7.   MARKET COMPETITION, PARENTAL CHOICE AND INDIVIDUAL
     SELF-MANAGEMENT ARE REDEFINING HOW SCHOOLS RELATE
     TO THEIR WIDER ENVIRONMENTS.

> *Decentralization can sweep away bureaucracy, but it often removes local professional support as well.*

Although schooling is becoming more centralized in some respects, through the proliferation of curriculum targets, learning standards and achievement tests, their day-to-day management and responsibility for meeting quality standards and performance goals is increasingly a matter for individual school determination. Schools are having to become more market conscious, more competitive for "clients", more preoccupied with image and public relations. School councils or parent councils and charter schools have been widely legislated as one way to push schools in this direction of market consciousness and client responsiveness. It is clear that such councils are turning teachers and principals outwards toward wider publics as they plan, present and defend what they teach. However, the benefits of all this for students are not always so clear.

Market competition and school self-management may make teachers more diligent in courting parental support and involvement. They may even urge teachers to work more closely with their immediate colleagues to ensure the success and survival of their own school. But this kind of institutional competitiveness also divides schools and their teachers from each other. Decentralization can sweep away bureaucracy, but it often removes local professional support as well. Teachers have little incentive to work with and learn from colleagues in other schools when their schools are in competition for clients.

An unintended consequence of the self-managing school movement is that it may create huge vacuums of professional development at the local level. For example, in England, where self-managing schools have been in existence for many years, teachers' opportunities to attend local professional meetings in their school district, or to attend professional development sessions where they can exchange views and experiences with colleagues from elsewhere have decreased. In one recent study, Helsby & Knight (1997) found that lessened opportunity for cross-school collaboration coupled with pressures to compete have resulted in insular school-based activities.

So how can we fill the professional development vacuum that the moves towards self-management often create? We must search for new and better ways to enable teachers to learn from their colleagues in other schools, so they can belong in a real sense to a wider profession, with all the wisdom and learning it has to offer. Making connections outside one's own school is a multifaceted task, not one that is confined to the immediate neighbourhood or community.

8. SCHOOLS CAN NO LONGER BE INDIFFERENT TO WHAT KINDS OF LIVING AND WORKING AWAIT THEIR STUDENTS WHEN THEY MOVE INTO THE ADULT WORLD.

What's out there in the changing economy is also inside students' heads, in their anxieties and aspirations.

When students leave school or even university, there is no immediate work for many of them anymore, or the work is very different than it used to be. The economies of the developed world are in turmoil. Restructuring and downsizing are pervasive. Bridges (1994:5) comments that after the U.S. recession of the late 1980s and early 1990s, only 18% of the lost jobs had returned. In other recessions, the jobs eventually came back. This time, he says, the message is clear, "jobs are going away, not just until times improve but for good." More than this, he observes, the way we package work into discrete, well-defined, lifelong bundles called jobs is itself a fading phenomenon.

Similarly, in his study of 'How the New Economy is Changing Our Lives' in Canada, Reid (1996) discredits several powerful economic myths including:

- growth is good for everyone;
- science and technology will save us;

- a good education means a good job; *and*

- the public interest still counts.

In their blistering attack on corporate criticisms of Canadian education, Barlow and Robertson (1994:69) note that between 1989 and 1993, permanent plant closures accounted for 65% of all layoffs. Yet less than one quarter of layoffs were caused by such closures during the 1981-82 recession. Ironically, they conclude, "while it is easy to find many examples of business criticizing education's "failures," it is much more difficult to find concrete promises of real jobs by the corporate community" (p. 61).

Part-time work, temporary work and contracting out are the new ingredients of corporate flexibility. Their rapid growth is challenging our traditional conceptions of what work is and how it is organized, along with our relationships to employers, and the importance we attach to paid work within our wider lives. Handy (1994) notes that for more and more young people, paid permanent work will start later in their lives and finish sooner, compared to their parents' generation.

When the world of work becomes so totally unreliable some want schools to wash their hands of the business connection. But this makes no sense. Students are as aware as anyone of the changing economic realities. They know that pieces of paper no longer provide automatic passports to security or success. The job lights are dimming at the end of the educational tunnel and this is leading students to question their work ethic and the relevance of what their schools offer them. What's "out there" in the changing economy is also inside students' heads, in their anxieties and aspirations. We should critique these changing work realities as we connect with them, but we can't turn back the clock to simpler schooling for simpler times and ignore them.

Others want closer connections between schooling and work. They advocate partnerships with industry, corporate investment in education, business involvement in the curriculum, more student placements on work experience, putting more emphasis in schools on the skills that business requires, and restructuring the management and organization of schooling along similar lines to the restructuring that has taken place elsewhere. These kinds of connections can provide a treasure chest of stimuli for learning. Or they can be a Pandora's box of corporate 'hype' and financial expediency. What's worth fighting for beyond your school, therefore, is not just building partnerships with business, but creating partnerships that are morally defensible and educationally worthwhile. Working well with business partners means opening their hearts and minds, not just their wallets.

Schools should not only connect with the workplace, but also put work in its place alongside the other things that young people aspire to and value. Wynn's (1994) extensive research in Australia shows that the aspirations of most youth are not only for worthwhile work but also for a decent life. For young people, she says:

> *Achieving adulthood involves getting a good job, as well as establishing intimate social relationships and participating at a political level. The main issue for the transition process is not just one of jobs, it is of establishing a livelihood.*

Indeed, the disappearance of jobs as we know them is leading many people to re-evaluate the place that work occupies in their lives – choosing where they work before what they work at and valuing their lifestyle choices alongside or above their choices of career.

Clearly, there's a lot waiting "out there" for young people when they leave school which affects how they respond to what schools offer. Creating morally defensible connections with the working world and preparing young people for a wider livelihood that is satisfying and worthwhile, are two of the more fundamental things worth fighting for beyond our schools.

9. THE PRESSURES OF TODAY'S COMPLEX ENVIRONMENTS ARE
    RELENTLESS, AND CONTRADICTORY.

*Not all instances of chaos and uncertainty are accidental,
unintended or unavoidable.*

There is 'a new science of complexity' which says that the link between cause
and effect is increasingly difficult to trace; that change (planned or
otherwise) unfolds in non-linear ways; that paradoxes and contradictions
abound; and that creative solutions arise out of diversity, uncertainty and
chaos (Stacey, 1996). Because schools and school systems are scrutinized so
publicly they can become special victims of complex, rapidly changing
environments (and also special beneficiaries as we shall argue later). There
are several reasons for the increased chaos and complexity that educators
now face.

First, the instant access to information and heightened speed of
decision-making that have been created by new technologies, significantly
reduce our ability to foresee and control events. The result is greater anxiety
and stress. One way that people respond to all this uncertainty is by seeking
"the latest comprehensive recipe for success" (Stacey, 1996:7). These 'silver
bullets' may reduce anxiety temporarily, but eventually lead to long-term
cynicism when none of them work. Working effectively as educators with the
rapidly changing world outside school means abandoning these illusions of
administrative predictability and control.

A second cause of uncertainty and complexity in teachers' work also
arises from the increased speed of information flow and decision making.
Modern technology compresses time and space. The media present instant
stories and reaction to public policy announcements with such speed that
inaccuracies and superficial debate are common. Under these circumstances,
change strategies can degenerate into uncoordinated reflex reactions. A
principal of a secondary school described to us how being an educational
leader these days was like living in an endless present – always responding
to immediate and insistent pressures, with no time to think ahead or to reflect

on how things had gone already. Reflex reactions are superficial reactions. There have to be better ways of responding to the world beyond school than this.

Third, even the knowledge bases that guide our educational responses to complexity are unstable. Knowledge about classroom learning, effective leadership or planned change, for example, is constantly being challenged. Rapid circulation and wide availability of scientific information mean that findings begin to be overturned almost the moment they are released. We now work in worlds of great scientific uncertainty. Many of the truths of today are the half-truths or falsehoods of tomorrow. This is a curse, but also a blessing. Scientific uncertainty creates anxiety. Yet it also reduces our blind dependence on the proclamations of others. We have a chance to take change out of the hands of experts and place it in the laps of our communities, our colleagues and ourselves. From this vantage point we can relate to experts in a less dependent manner.

Fourth, greater diversities of culture, language and religion in our student populations are throwing traditional educational goals into question and making consensus difficult to achieve. Some people seek to solve this problem by creating schools of choice. Each cultural and religious group, they say, should be permitted to have its own schools, based on its own unique values. This solution accommodates the demands of difference but at the price of tolerance, working together and mutual understanding that are essential to the ideals of community and democracy. Other people respond to increased uncertainty and diversity by retreating to comfortable memories of the past. They long to return to schools with simple curricula and singular values as they remembered them thirty years or more ago. They are drawn to lost golden ages, to myths and illusions of ill-remembered pasts (Hargreaves, 1994). Nostalgia, it is worth noting, was originally regarded as an illness. The solutions it offers are unworkable with the diverse communities of today.

Fifth, not only are outside pressures and demands on teachers increasing, they are also contradictory. For example, advocates of greater curriculum relevance and teaching for understanding want to expose students to more socially controversial material which will help them develop critical thinking and problem-solving skills. Powerful pressure groups from the religious right do not want sacred truths and culturally conservative values to be questioned, so they push in the opposite direction. The pressures of cultural diversity are leading policy-makers to embrace multiple intelligences and varied learning styles, while parents and some employers' groups agitating for "quality" education want greater standardization. Teachers may find that their principals and school districts subscribe to whole-language methodologies, whereas many of the parents of their students who come from other cultures may feel that more didactic approaches to teaching reading are better. Policy makers are often too faint-hearted to choose between these different ideological directions. So they frequently fudge them – creating policies that are ambiguous and contradictory. Teachers have the unenviable job of dealing with the consequences.

How are teachers to cope with these contradictions? Some comply with the pressures of the stronger group and ignore those that are less pressing. Others veer incoherently and chaotically from one demand to the next – teaching to cross-curricular outcomes at one moment, and filling in traditional report cards the next. Then there are those who try to appease all groups by making their teaching and curriculum as inoffensive and innocuous (and consequently as uninteresting) as possible. All these responses are educationally unsatisfactory. They concede influence to those with the greatest power and strongest voice, and create incoherence and inconsistency in the curriculum.

Not all instances of chaos and uncertainty are accidental, unintended or unavoidable. Some of it is manufactured by governmental and corporate power to maximize their interests of tax reduction and social control by keeping labour forces flexible, interest groups fragmented and everyone off-balance. Berliner & Biddle (1996) in the United States, and Barlow & Robertson (1994) in Canada have described how across the world, myths of falling standards, feckless teachers and failing schools have been used to destabilize public confidence in education and provide pretexts for widespread political impositions of educational reform. This kind of manufactured chaos should be attacked, not accommodated.

Yet in their study of school administrators' responses to powerful social change forces like poverty, new technologies and changing labour markets, in five school districts, Levin and Riffel (1997) conclude that schools and school systems:

- do not really know how to respond to the changes they experience;

- have developed no systematic ways of learning about the nature and implications of the social changes around them;

- have limited and unimaginative strategies for responding to change;

- have perceptions and reactions that are dominated by conventional wisdom, with the result that they try familiar (but unsuccessful) solutions, or low-risk one-of-a-kind initiatives that have little impact on the larger system; *and*

- possess a weak outward-looking stance.

It is time for teachers and schools to take greater initiative; to adopt coherent and collective moral stands in relation to these pressures; to represent children's interest in the political tussle for education, when children cannot represent their own. Many teachers and their organizations now do this. But answering critics by hanging on to existing practice and defending the status quo is not enough. Teachers' stance towards assessment and standards policy is a good case in point. Teachers rightly object to achievement data being used in crude and misleading ways to rank schools in published league tables of performance (taking no account of the different kinds of communities in which these schools are placed). Yet there is no use trying to keep the lid on performance data. Instead, the most effective teachers wade into the fray contesting what is misleading, and creating more meaningful, well-rounded school profiles to communicate what goes on in their classrooms. You can run but you cannot hide from the chaotic and complex environments surrounding schools today.

10. OUR EXISTING STRUCTURES ARE EXHAUSTED.

We have seen that teachers now work in contexts of great diversity, complexity and uncertainty. Yet existing school structures do not enable them to respond as they should. Many teachers are having to learn to teach in ways they were not taught themselves. Teachers' formal responsibilities are with whole classes, but many of their tasks in assessment and student-centered learning are with individuals and small groups. Many secondary school teachers are being asked not only to teach their subjects but also to be guides and mentors for individual students' personal and career development. Parents clamour for more information about their children's progress, but contact is often restricted to a few awkward minutes with each teacher a couple of times a year. School structures and cultures are ill designed for teachers to meet the needs of all students, to have worthwhile discussions with parents, and even to work with each other. Existing structures and cultures make it agonizingly difficult for schools to respond effectively to what's "out there".

Ontario's Royal Commission on Learning (1995) concluded that if there is one theme "out there" it is "that Ontario's schools aren't equipped to deal with the future" (p. 3). The National Commission on the Future of Teaching in America (1996) similarly concludes that school structures are hopelessly outdated:

> Today's schools are organized in ways that support neither student nor teacher learning well. Like the turn-of-the-century industries they were modeled after – most of which are now redesigning themselves – current structures were designed to mimic factories that used semi-skilled workers to do discrete pieces of work in a mass production assembly line (p. 45).

According to the Commission, schools "use time nonproductively" "use staff nonproductively," and "use money, nonproductively." Too many educators and parents are locked into existing structures where anything other than individual teachers in separate classes, students graded by age, a curriculum organized into subjects and divided into lesson periods, secondary-school department heads vetting and vetoing any changes that might threaten their interests, and parents being contacted only at specified times in the year – is not considered to be 'real school' at all (Metz, 1990).

It is exhausting to use strategies of active and cooperative learning in a series of episodic subject periods. It is unreasonable to expect teachers to counsel or conference with individual students while leaving the rest of the class to fend for themselves. Existing structures tie teachers to inappropriate time frames. Isolating them within their classes insulates them from potential sources of in-class help: from fellow teachers, student teachers, parent helpers and other resources in the community.

Teachers who really value their emotional bonds to students are willing to experiment with alternative structures that make these bonds stronger. One Grade 8 teacher who was beginning to work with a schedule divided into bigger blocks of time, put it like this:

> I can help any kid learn anything as long as he is motivated and I feel that I can motivate the kid through reality, natural situations. But in order to do that I have to be able to have block periods of time to setup situations where I can show them the reality of this and to me that's a great thing. I get rolling on something and if the kids get rolling on something I don't want to be stopped by a bell telling me to move on, so I welcome it.

> (Hargreaves & Earl, 1997)

When teachers really put students and their connections to students first, structural changes often follow very close behind. But without structural change, community pressures and educational innovations just overwhelm them.

Structures that support teaching and learning, and that involve parents and others in supporting teaching and learning, cannot be changed by teachers themselves or by teachers keeping to themselves. Parents and others outside the school must also challenge the existing organization of schooling. They must support unfamiliar structures that will actually help teachers to bring about positive change, and spare their energies in doing so. This is a monumental task of professional and community learning. A number of districts are now working on creating new in-built infrastructures in the school, the system and the community to support continuous learning and problem-solving (Fullan & Watson, 1997). Establishing radically new infrastructures and cultures of learning and teaching that are up to the task of working in the turbulent environments described in these pages – is one of the most essential things worth fighting for within and beyond our schools.

The Challenge

Parents must acknowledge that the schooling, which will be best for their children in the 21st century, must be very different from the schooling they experienced themselves.

The forces of change we have described are already evident within countless classrooms, in the characteristics of the children, in the problems and new potential they bring to the school, and in the way in which local and national interest groups make their presence known. Within these challenging and complex times, teachers must find more and better ways to work with others in the interests of students. They must define their sense of professionalism so that it does not place them above or set them apart from parents and the wider public, but gives them the confidence and courage to engage openly with others. Moreover, they must do this even when the conditions do not initially favour such action.

This does not, and should not, mean teachers running themselves into the ground with extra work beyond the responsibilities they already have. What needs to change in schools is how people work, not how much they work. The structures that have separated schools from the surrounding community have made the work more difficult. In fact, they have made it impossible.

Teachers should not be left alone in this quest. Parents must acknowledge that the schooling which will be best for their children in the 21st century, must be very different from the schooling they experienced themselves. They must let go of their attachments to old versions of schooling, and abandon nostalgic longings for ill-remembered pasts. They must certainly expect a lot of their children's teachers, but should base this on understanding, courtesy and partnership. Criticism and questioning is more palatable when it is accompanied by positive feedback, concrete help and active support. If parents expect teachers to change, they must show they are willing to change too.

In describing what's "out there" we have painted a picture of immense complexity. It is also one of tremendous excitement and possibility. Building community, protecting democracy, making education a public good as well as a private one, using new technologies to deepen learning, creating high quality education in contexts of great diversity – these things define the moral purpose of schooling for a society where sophisticated knowledge and skills will make young people economically productive, and where civic commitments will make them democratically responsible and active. Educators can only do all this, if individually and with others, they 'go deeper' and 'go wider'. Once they do, the teaching profession will never be quite the same again.

Chapter 2
GOING DEEPER

Morality does not soar on its own wings.

Amitai Etzioni (The Spirit of Community, 1995)

Going deeper means hard thinking and soul searching about the fundamental value and purpose of what we do as educators. It means reaching into our hearts to care more deeply for those we teach and to forge stronger emotional bonds with other people, such as parents, who share in this educational responsibility. Going deeper means staying optimistic and hanging on to hope, even in the most difficult circumstances, not as a futile indulgence, but as an active commitment that helps make real differences in young people's lives. Going deeper, in other words, involves purpose, passion, and hope.

Purpose

In What's Worth Fighting For? Working Together for Your School, we talked about the importance of the teacher's purpose, and how policy makers and administrators often overlooked it when they tried to change their schools. Many reformers still have to learn that teachers will not commit to a change if they cannot see the point of it. We showed how the prime satisfactions for teachers are not monetary rewards or abstract results, but the joys of interacting with children and the differences they can make to students' lives. We talked about needing to respect the care and relationships that are central to teachers' work, and about not losing sight of these or letting them be crowded out by other reform emphases. Conversely, we also warned against treating all teachers' existing purposes as sacrosanct. In a changing world, a healthy school is one where teachers constantly revisit and renew their purposes; always looking for evidence and feedback about how well they are doing, and honestly examining whether they need to do things differently or better.

Reaching out to parents and communities beyond the school is more difficult these days because it is harder, much harder, to reach students themselves. Far too many reform efforts fail to come to grips with this. They talk confidently, even arrogantly, about standards and targets; about packing the curriculum with more science and mathematics; about ranking schools competitively in league tables of academic performance; or about repeatedly inspecting them to check that they are up to the mark. How all this will make a difference for students or help teachers reach their students better is much less clear.

Meanwhile, because schools are having to compete for "clients," student expulsions are rising as schools' images and performance records are put before the needs of troubled adolescents. Discipline problems and bullying in the early years of secondary school are also on the rise in some places, as studying specialist subjects with many different teachers is given precedence over having students work with just a few teachers who they know well and feel they can turn to. Alienated adolescents do not make academically successful students. If there is one factor that stands out as students move through the years from elementary to secondary schools it is the increasing percentage who are seriously disengaged from their own learning. You can't teach students if you can't reach them. Standards-obsessed reformers have not yet got this point. Their sense of purpose is seriously askew. All head and no heart!

Some critics have tried to rectify this situation. Teachers and schools should have a moral purpose, they say. But they present few ideas about what exactly the purposes should be. Going deeper means getting clear and coming clean about purposes. Not any purpose will do. Schools should reach for higher educational purposes which truly are moral in transforming children's lives and building a better world for the generations of the future. Among the many purposes of schooling, four stand out to us as having special moral value: to love and care, to serve, to empower and, of course, to learn.

1. TO LOVE AND CARE

> *For many students establishing relationships of respect and care is a necessary foundation for intellectual as well as social development.*

As the song says, "what's love got to do with it?" In the previous chapter, we showed how finding love and forming relationships are among young people's most important life ambitions. Schools, where learning leaves little place for love, are schools without substance or soul. We are not saying that it is easy to care for all students, especially when they show an active disrespect for teachers, or a sullen lack of interest day after day in the classroom. We do say that it won't be standards, technology, curriculum or new designs for schools that will get at the root of the problem, *unless they are also accompanied by new relationships between teachers and students*. To teach effectively you have to have an overriding purpose, such as Fried's (1995) science teacher who says:

> *I believe I make a difference not only by helping kids connect math and science to their lives, but also in understanding how to reach their goals in life.*

Goleman (1995) points out that empathy is one of the most funda-mental attributes of what he calls *emotional intelligence*. Empathy established in the early years of childhood – the ability to understand another's anger, share their joy or feel their sorrow – lays the foundations for a strong sense of social justice in adolescence and adulthood; when empathy towards others becomes generalized to entire social groups who are poor, marginalized, discriminated against or oppressed. Uncaring and unconcerned citizens come from emotionally stunted families and schools. Emotional intelligence involves being aware of and able to express emotions, to empathize effectively with the emotional states of others, and to manage and moderate our emotions so they do not consume or overwhelm us (so that anger does not turn into rage or sadness into despair).

Schools do not pay enough attention to emotional intelligence, says Goleman. He shows that emotional intelligence is not a soft option in schooling, a distraction from the hard challenges of *real* learning. Instead, it actually adds value to cognitive achievement and subsequent success in adult life. Some aspects of emotional intelligence such as "self-control, zeal and persistence and the ability to motivate oneself" (Goleman, 1995: xii) are essential to long-run cognitive achievement. Indeed, successfully arousing appropriate emotions moves us and motivates us to want to learn more and achieve better. The capacities to form positive relationships, empathize with others' concerns and care about their lives are powerful leadership assets in many walks of life. Goleman himself concludes:

> *Much evidence testifies that people who are emotionally adept – who know and manage their own feelings well, and who read and deal effectively with other people's feelings well – are at an advantage in any domain of life, whether romance and intimate relationships or picking up the unspoken rules that govern success in organizational politics. People with well-developed emotional skills are also more likely to be content and effective in their lives, mastering the habits of mind that foster their own productivity; people who cannot marshal some control over their emotional life fight inner battles that sabotage their ability for focused work and clear thought.*
>
> (Goleman, 1995:36).

Many schools are poor cultivators of emotional intelligence. They give love and care much too low a priority. Noddings (1992) observes in her ground-breaking book on *The Challenge to Care in Schools:*

> *the single greatest complaint of students in schools is, "They don't care" . . . They feel alienated from their school work, separated from the adults who try to teach them, and adrift in a world perceived as baffling and hostile. At the same time, most teachers work very hard and express deep concern for their students. In an important sense, teachers do care, but they are unable to make the connections that would complete caring relationships with their students (p. 2).*

Dropout students report that the one factor which might have prevented them leaving school early was the feeling that there was one adult in the school who knew them well and cared for them (Hargreaves, Earl & Ryan, 1996).

Sizer (1992) argues that in order to be able to love and care for students properly, no teacher should teach more than 80 students a week – yet the subject organization of secondary schools gives most teachers much higher student-contact loads. Many educational reforms cram the curriculum with more and more targets or content, but leave little or no place for care.

Somehow, many teachers can and do overcome these limitations. The most creative and emotionally engaged teachers see themselves not just as educating learners and workers, but as developing citizens. Some teachers even profess love for their students. In our study of Grade 7 and 8 teachers, one of them said:

> I love children. I love all ages. I have a great deal of trouble with teachers who say "Oh I only like Grade 1's. I won't teach anybody else. All other kids are awful." That makes my back just raise right up. I think to myself, "if you don't like kids, you shouldn't be teaching." You have to like kids. You have to like what you are doing a lot, and I do.

Teachers in this study were not naive romantics. The one quoted above was often tired and frustrated and felt sick the morning she was interviewed. Another confessed that he felt like strangling his students some days. But it was "the kids; that's what keeps you going – I mean, if you can only help one in your year, that's what makes it all worthwhile."

Teachers liked to celebrate stories of their efforts with individuals, and what they had learned from them. One spoke of a "wonderful boy" who had just arrived from the United States, for whom she had had to make a wide range of curriculum adjustments. Another told of a girl who had "started off completely lost at the beginning of the year" yet who, after involvement in self-evaluation, reflected that "I'm doing so much better and I feel really good, but I don't want to feel conceited." Another teacher described a previously "struggling" child who had responded exceptionally well to an integrated unit on flight, had constructed the most effective airplane, and had revealed that he'd been making airplanes since Grade 1.

Ensuring that all students felt included and no one was treated as an "outcast" really mattered to the teachers in this study. They cared deeply about special education students, but not through pity or over-protectiveness. They were particularly pleased when special needs children were successfully integrated with the others. "I love the fact that they are sitting in groups right now, working with everybody else", said one. Another commented, "it was really neat to see" a colleague enter the classroom and have "no idea who the (special education) kids were and she couldn't tell you which one was identified and which one was just your high academic student." Integrating students, making them feel included, took a lot of work, as when one teacher created resource packs of mathematics and writing strategies for all students, even though the special education students needed them most. Teaching like this is hard labour, but for those who do it, it is a labour of love.

When love and care extend to inclusion, this advances the interests of equity and social justice as well. The Grade 7/8 teachers saw multicultural diversity, for example, as a great educational opportunity, not a worrisome obstacle. When teachers taught about the Holocaust, they could connect it to the lives of children whose relatives had died in other wars in Somalia, Vietnam, or Japan. When a mathematics class included a Kurdish student who used a different system of division, this enabled the class to explore cultural differences in the use of "order of operation" in ways that included many people's mathematical experiences and heightened the sophistication of overall mathematical understanding at the same time. For the teachers in this study, tolerance, respect and fairness were moral virtues and values that underpinned all their teaching – and it was the love and care of relating to students that in turn gave these virtues a foundation and held them together.

Recall Patricia Murphy, the special education teacher from Ottawa whose words opened our book? Each September she cuts out apples and makes a tree, and inscribes the names of her students on the apples so that at the beginning of the school year "when we climb the stairs to the room to begin our ten-month journey together, they will see their names on the door and know that I expect them, that I'm glad they're here, that we all belong to each other now." The second week of September last year, one of the students ripped the tree off the door and tore it to shreds before he ran out of the classroom screaming that he hated this place and that no one could make him come back. As she makes the tree this year, the memory returns:

I smile, remember it now, because he did come back, with only a little coaxing. And in a few months, he started to read, mastered the dreaded nine-times table, and earned himself a spot on the track and field team. He even smiled occasionally.

None of this denies the importance of knowledge and cognitive development. It says that for many students establishing relationships of respect and care is a necessary foundation for intellectual as well as social development. If you think that this applies only to elementary students you haven't grasped what 's wrong with secondary schools. We need all teachers to be intellectually inspiring – to be passionate about subjects and ideas. But they must also want and know how to teach "beyond the front row" (Dryden, 1995). Doing this means learning to develop relationships with students who are not eager to learn as well as those that are. In Japan, even with traditional teaching styles and classes of 45 or more, teachers devote extraordinary effort to establishing a strong emotional bond or "ligature" with each and every student. For them, this is the foundation of all discipline and learning (Shimahara & Sakai, 1995).

We don't deny that some students will turn out to be unreachable. But if teachers revisited or reawakened their moral purpose, and regrouped the school and their collective teaching to work on relationships with all students, things would improve dramatically. What if, by doing this, instead of connecting with a third of the class, they now related effectively to two-thirds? What if, of these two-thirds, the majority also took some responsibility for changing the student learning culture?

Once teachers really put a priority on care, justice and inclusiveness as moral purposes underpinning their teaching, everything starts to change. Impelled by the moral purposes of caring and building relationships, the Grades 7 and 8 teachers we mentioned earlier, preferred school structures with large blocks of time where they could pursue a subject in depth, maintain the "flow" of a lesson, or continue discussing something of personal importance to students, without the bell truncating the relationship by calling a halt to the lesson. Some teachers (like those in countries such as Denmark) preferred to stay with their classes year after year to maintain the emotional bond in which good teaching could flourish. They frowned on "efficient" but impersonal, computer-coded report cards, and instead supported more authentic communication with parents that was extensive, reciprocal, spoken more than written, and included students rather than keeping them at a distance. When care, justice and inclusiveness become active purposes and commitments in education, teaching and learning look very different. So do the relationships that teachers have with students and their parents.

Where do parents figure in all this? What is *their* moral responsibility? We should not be any less demanding of parents' moral responsibility than we are of teachers'. Going deeper also implicates parents. It should not all be off-loaded on to the school.

It's hard being a parent these days. Exposed to graphically violent images in the media, and confronted early in life by information and advice about how to say "no" to drugs, how to distinguish good touch from bad touch, and how to be especially watchful of strangers, children are being robbed of their innocence. Being a parent is hardest of all when you are poor. Nourishing your children properly, helping them to remain hopeful, keeping your own spirits up, finding time to care for them when you have to work night shift or put two or three jobs together just to make ends meet would tax the soul of most adults. Levin & Riffel (1997) have shown that the educational and behavioural problems which many school administrators attribute to family breakdown and single parenthood are really problems of poverty. Many single parents are also financially disadvantaged parents. Governments (and their supporters) who willingly trade welfare for taxes, as well as corporations who employ and exploit the working poor have a lot to answer for here.

Governments can do more, much more, to support families. One way is to lower the age at which publicly funded schooling begins, especially in communities experiencing great social and economic difficulty. Good quality early childhood education helps single parents put their lives back together, and is one of the best predictors of improved literacy, lower rates of school dropout and lowered incidences of delinquency and criminality in later life (Ontario Royal Commission on Learning, 1994; OECD, 1997).

A first class system of early childhood education is the hallmark of a caring and civilized society whose government is driven by a sense of deep moral purpose, along with an eye for long-term stability and efficiency.

Yet, in addition to the obligations of government, schools can and should make their own mark on the poverty problem. At the moment, as Levin & Riffel (1997) found, their responses while worthy, are fragmented add-ons to what schools already do – breakfast clubs, winter clothing drives, etc. The best solutions involve changing the core of what schools do. Two such solutions are:

> Ensure that disadvantaged students receive as challenging a level of instruction as other students . . . this means moving away from pull-out programmes and curriculum with lower expectations . . .

> A much stronger connection with parents, families and communities. This strategy assures that the school . . . must work closely with parents and others to ensure not only that schools are good places for young people, but that the school contributes to the overall economic and social welfare of the community (p. 130-131).

To make a real difference in the learning and lives of disadvantaged students especially, the purpose of love and care cannot be regarded as a soft option, or be pushed to the periphery of the system. Effective love and care is tough stuff. It involves schools, teachers and parents dramatically reshaping the heart of what they do.

It is not just poor parents who are having difficulty establishing supportive conditions for their children's development. Etzioni (1995) argues that in the last thirty years or so, we have generally allowed children to be devalued. Many parents have been so busy "making it", they have left hardly any time to devote to their family and relationships. "Quality time" has become a yuppie euphemism for hardly any time at all. How can you praise your children when they do well, if you're never around to see them doing it? Young children are expected to be less innocent, increasingly independent and self-reliant, not because of their own needs, but to satisfy the needs of their busy parents to be involved in something else.

In the middle to upper echelons of the socio-economic scale many parents could make better choices between climbing as rapidly as possible up the career ladder by putting in more hours at the office, and dedicating more time to their children; between spending money on their children or spending time with them. Here the really deep issue, of which increased divorce rates may be just one indicator, is whether too many parents – men and women alike – have become excessively preoccupied with their own self-fulfillment, career quests and life projects to the detriment of their children's needs. Some parents appear so obsessed with "finding themselves" they are losing their children along the way. This, incidentally, may be one reason why many qualified leaders are starting to refuse promotions. The moral costs to their children and their own lives are seen to be simply too high.

Hochschild (1997) has studied the "time bind" which corporate office workers and executives experience as they struggle to meet the emotional needs of their families while putting in more and more hours at work. Some parents, she observes, emotionally *downsize* their families by assuming that children will be better off if they are more independent. Some *outsource* emotional tasks to contracted services like babysitters. Regardless of intent, emotional engagement in the family is increasingly being diminished, says Hochschild.

We have to ask then, along with Steinberg (1996), "If so many parents really want their child to do well in school, why do only a minority of parents do what they ought to be doing?" (p. 103). One answer is that it is exceedingly difficult to create a home atmosphere conducive to positive child development. It involves combining approaches that don't easily go together: acceptance (vs. rejection), firmness (vs. leniency), and autonomy (vs. control). The integration of acceptance, firmness and autonomy in parenting is complex and demanding work. Steinberg (1996) describes parents who practise this combination well as "authoritative". The ability to work with these paradoxes of parenting distinguishes "good parents from bad ones" (p. 106).

Steinberg says that despite good intentions, nearly one in three parents end up being disengaged from their children:

Disengaged parents have for one reason or another, "checked out" of child-rearing. They have disengaged from responsibilities of parental discipline – they do not know how their child is doing in school, have no idea who their child's friends are, and are not aware of how their child spends his or her free time – but they have also disengaged from being accepting and supportive as well. They rarely spend time in activities with their child, and seldom just talk with their adolescent about the day's events (p. 188).

Parent-school connections can counter the problem to some extent. Neighbourhoods and communities can also make a difference:

Adolescents who live in neighbourhoods in which a large proportion of families are authoritative [combine acceptance, firmness, autonomy] perform better in school and are less likely to get into trouble than adolescents who come from identical home environments – and who go to the same school – but who live in neighbourhoods in which the population of authoritative families is much lower (p. 153).

In summary, a variety of social factors conspire to make it extremely difficult to engage a large proportion of our children in any meaningful learning at school. We won't be able to do everything at once, but the direction of the solution is pretty clear.

- We need to involve students in talking about what makes learning difficult for them, what diminishes motivation, and engagement, and what makes some give up or settle for minimum effort (Rudduck, et al, 1996:3).

- We need to commit to and insist on early childhood intervention – to shape the twig so the tree will not grow twisted (OECD, 1997).

- We need to foster and support caring teaching, to build stronger bonds for better learning and improved opportunity (Dryden, 1995; Fried, 1995).

- We need to build relationships between teachers and parents that involve learning and caring on both sides (Epstein, 1995; Steinberg, 1996).

- We need to ensure that school structures and timetables support the purpose of care instead of squeezing it to the margins (Hargreaves, Earl, & Ryan, 1996).

Going deep in these ways can be done individually – to a point. It is much more powerful when it involves partnerships and mutual learning among students, teachers and parents.

2. TO SERVE

Service to others should be one of the most basic purposes of family life and schooling.

Morality does not emerge by itself. It "does not soar on its own wings" (Etzioni, 1993:31). We get our moral bearings and develop our moral commitments through the communities we join and belong to. The family is the first of these.

When they function well as moral communities, families are not only places where children are loved and learn to love but also places where they learn the virtues (and the satisfactions) of duty, service, obligation and commitment to people and purposes beyond themselves. Negotiation, patience, settling conflicts, sharing out chores, and serving others' needs as well as (and sometimes before) one's own are some of the moral virtues that children pick up when families work well as communities.

In many financially comfortable homes, shared community seems to be less important than individual autonomy. Teenagers' bedrooms have turned into self-sustaining biospheres – each with its own computer, music centre, television and telephone. This certainly enhances adolescents' independence, but it also adds to their isolation. They have little need to communicate with other family members (to negotiate which television programmes to watch together, for example).

In these families, the price of technological and physical *independence* (having your own space) may be some loss of human *interdependence*. Common meal-times are one of the casualties. Families are less inclined to sit down, eat and talk together now than to graze the bread box, the microwave and the fridge, like independent species. Are these concessions to adolescent consumer autonomy really made in the best moral interests of adolescents themselves? With busy work lives and tightly scheduled leisure activities, time spent together as a family rarely occurs naturally these days. It must be protected and worked for. Families must put community before convenience – at least some of the time.

If this talk of duty and service sounds like a nostalgic preoccupation with middle class manners, consider the following story told to one of us by an Ontario elementary teacher. Asked to describe a recent experience with a student that was emotionally positive for her, she talked about a 7-year old girl in her class who had been raised for much of her early childhood by her homeless mother on the streets of the city. The girl's father had been in jail and would be deported on his release. So she was taken in by her mother's sister. "If my aunt didn't get me, I'd probably be dead by now," the 7-year old reflected. Though a busy, single parent, this aunt spent a lot of time with her seven year old niece, who became a bright and kind girl at home and school as a result.

The teacher's class became involved in a food drive and children were asked to bring in items to be delivered to food banks for the poor. The teacher was saddened that one or two of her more comfortably-off class members procrastinated about bringing in their food-bank contributions, offering the excuse that their mothers forgot to put the food in their backpacks for them! By contrast, the 7-year old girl related to her teacher how she had gone home and described the food drive to her aunt. They talked a lot about it together, she said, and while they decided they didn't have a lot of money "we could all give one thing." So they looked in their cupboard and brought out two tins of pork and beans – their own contribution to the food drive. The teacher reflected how the girl had demonstrated, far better than she herself ever could, the real meaning and importance of giving, charity and love.

Families as communities must not only give love to their children, but also make demands on them. For it is in this way that the value of service, of contributing to a wider community, is first learned and embraced. Today's fast paced and fractured family in which autonomy prevails over community is due for a reappraisal. It is up to many parents to start taking a lead in this. If schools are going to liaise better with the home, there have to be better homes with which to liaise.

After the family, most children's next meaningful community is the school. In the previous chapter, we argued that schools are one of our last hopes for rebuilding a sense of community, and that a civic-minded public school system is essential for democracy. Saul (1995) worried about the "adoration of self-interest and our denial of the public good" (p. 2). Reid (1996:250) says that when only the free market economy is the driver:

> *Forgotten or ignored are the problems that can develop when people operating in nobody's interest but their own secure a stranglehold on the way things are run.*

One of the primary purposes of education in a democracy is "to develop a broader sense of community and indeed in the world at large" (Saul, 1995:138.) Everywhere in education this purpose is weak or under threat. The official and "hidden" curriculum – not just social studies, but the entire way the school population lives on a daily basis – must model values and practices that build a strong sense of community. Self respect, caring for others, helping friends, respecting the views of others, being involved in the community are all values in danger of erosion, but fundamental to the moral purpose of our schools.

Service to others should be one of the most basic purposes of family life and schooling. Too often these days, time for volunteerism has to give way to official "curriculum" or to individualistic pursuits. When both parents and teachers acknowledge that students have obligations as well as entitlements, when schools and homes are places of love and duty together, then the chances for constructive dialogue between home and school are great indeed. But when parents are concerned only about their children's rights, and teachers want to talk only about students' compliance and obligations, then conflict between home and school over issues like discipline is extremely likely. Building better partnerships between home and school means strengthening the moral purposes of love, respect, service and care in each of these places. Without this moral deepening, home-school partnerships will collapse in bitter conflicts between indulgent parents and indifferent schools.

Developing meaning and commitment to abstract ideals like the public good begins with serving, caring and meeting obligations in one's immediate community, neighbourhood and school. Large ripples need only small stones. Cooperative learning, peer-mediated conflict resolution, cross-age tutoring, community service, home-school partnerships, school-work projects are only a few of the daily practices that can make a contribution in this direction. Giving 'at risk' students (and not just high achieving ones) significant responsibilities in caring for younger children, showing visitors around the school, and involving them in participating in school decisions deepen these practices still further. Community participation and leadership should include all students, not just the academically accomplished.

These values aren't just important for students to learn. Teachers and parents, we have shown, must also build collaborative cultures of reciprocal learning among themselves and with their students or else learning to serve cannot possibly be accomplished.

Moreover, these practices connect to an even larger purpose. Education of citizenry for the common good is seen as the main tool for democracy in previously closed societies engaged in transformation to more openness; (for example, in the former communist countries in Eastern Europe, and in South Africa). It is no less important in Western democracies. Teachers with moral purpose provide both models and a means for establishing public education as a common good.

3.   TO EMPOWER

Mobilized properly, politics can be used to support and advance student learning, instead of being a distraction from it.

Power and politics are inescapable realities of school life. People neglect these realities at their peril. In his groundbreaking book on *The Culture of the School and the Problem of Change*, Seymour Sarason (1982) judged that "any non-trivial effort at institutional change that is insensitive to the issue of power courts failure" (p. 89).

> *The school culture, like that of any other major social institution is political . . . Introducing, sustaining and assessing an educational change are political processes because they inevitably alter or threaten to alter existing power relationships, especially if that process implies, and always does, a reallocation of resources. Few myths have been as resistant to change as that which assumes that the culture of the school is a nonpolitical one (pp. 70-71).*

Many teachers want little to do with educational politics. Like people generally, they see politics as the domain of those who are cynical, self-seeking, opportunistic and manipulative. Most teachers don't see their work like this. For them, it is a virtuous calling, untainted by politics.

Although widely held, this view of politics shows only one face of it. Power and politics are not only inescapable, but also important parts of teaching. Mobilized properly, politics can be used to support and advance student learning, instead of being a distraction from it. Politics need not be used to establish power over people. It can be harnessed to build power with them – within school and beyond it. In this respect, we argue that empowering others – students, colleagues, parents and communities – should be one of the most central moral purposes of schooling.

In *What's Worth Fighting For? Working Together for Your School*, we argued that principals and school systems needed to empower their teachers more – engaging in decision-making, participating in team leadership, having a stake in developing the basic purposes and not just the technical delivery of education. High quality learning, we said, depended on more and deeper kinds of professional collaboration.

However, as Blase and Anderson (1995:130) point out "to empower teachers in isolation from parents, students and other stakeholders is to risk empowering one constituency at the price of disempowering others." We must ensure that by giving more voice to teachers, we don't ironically silence or marginalize the voices of others. As we said earlier, we need to build new kinds of professionalism that connect teachers with, rather than elevate them above, others in their school and community.

Empowerment must begin in the classroom. Sarason (1990) has said that most educational reforms fail because they simply do not address the existing power relationships of the classroom. This is the place where democratic community must start.

There are many ways in which the purposes of empowerment can be, and sometimes already are, developed in our classrooms. Teaching about power and democracy, not through dry coverage of content, but through simulation, outside visits, community participation and so on, is one clear approach (Meier, 1987). Direct involvement of students, all kinds of students, in governance and decision-making is another. But what matters most of all is how far students are empowered in their own classroom learning. The Grade 7 and 8 teachers we referred to created classroom environments where children felt comfortable asking questions or presenting an alternative point of view, where they had learning standards clearly explained to them, where they participated in brainstorming topics and ideas for integrated study, where they were given more responsibility for their own learning and its monitoring, and where they were integral participants in and contributors to parent-teacher interviews. Empowerment of students begins with the learning process itself.

We also need to empower parents and communities. This works best not just by involving more parent and community members in formal school governance – for in the vast majority of cases, professionals retain control of the key agendas, and community people simply defer to them. Nor does it work best by coordinating social service provision on the school site. Reviewing the research on this issue, Merz and Furman (1997:59) conclude that social service coordination "is primarily a connection *among professionals* across community agencies, rather than between schools and community members." Empowering parents, rather, means interacting with all of them more extensively, listening to them more sincerely, soliciting their opinions and feedback more determinedly, and involving them in curriculum development and in decisions about their own children's learning more widely – all on a regular basis.

Doing all this depends on great emotional security and considerable political skill and acuity among teachers. Creating positive politics that empowers students, parents and colleagues alike requires charm, diplomacy, self-mockery, guilelessness, coming down off one's pedestal, giving voice to others, actively soliciting criticism and dissent, searching for solutions instead of apportioning blame, involving others, encouraging them to take the lead, asking for their help, lobbying for support, building alliances, listening actively, and generally being able to "read" the micropolitics of the school.

To sum up: the moral purpose of schooling in a democracy is not just about service, love and caring entirely on professionals' own terms. It is about empowering students and parents as well.

4. TO LEARN

It is time we had a new kind of accountability in education – one that gets back to the moral basics of caring, serving, empowering and learning.

Learning and what we know about learning is also changing. As well as the "social" learning we have described so far, cognitive or intellectual learning is also undergoing a transformation. New approaches to teaching and learning focus on deep understanding, and the ability to apply knowledge in novel situations. These approaches are vital for creating a society that prospers from continuous learning and are revolutionary in what they imply for how teachers and students should go about learning. In this section we will describe three pillars of learning.

The first pillar involves the need to reshape learning experiences so that more students are engaged. This requires education that taps into their varied cultural backgrounds and beliefs and uses computers, not as toys or high-tech baby-sitting devices, but as tools to transform learning and increase young people's opportunities and life-chances.

George Lucas, of Star Wars fame, was deeply disturbed that his own experience in public school was frustrating and boring, yet in university and later life he pursued his dreams in a constant flow of learning and excitement of discovery and creativity: he wondered – "why can't school be interesting?" With the George Lucas Foundation, he set out to portray and capture what learning looks like when it is meaningful, absorbing and fun. The result is a video and document entitled *Live and Learn* (George Lucas Foundation, 1997). It contains all the elements of learning we talk about in this book: new approaches to l learning and teaching, assessment, technology, connecting to families, communities and businesses.

There is a revolutionary movement underway in cognitive science in which researchers are working with teachers and students in ordinary schools to change the nature of teaching and learning (Scardamalia & Bereiter, 1996; Gardner, 1991; Keating, 1995). Students and teachers are learning what it means to access expert knowledge, to construct their own understanding, and to apply what they know in creative ways. Young children, for example, are learning about airplanes by constructing a museum exhibition on the history of aviation, in which they access knowledge through technology and interaction with university physics professors and graduate students about theories of aerodynamics, and work with their hands and computers to create the exhibit (Scardamalia, 1997). Instances such as this exemplify the knowledge-building society and are revolutionary in how they redesign the pedagogy and conditions for learning. Of course, not all children in all schools can access expert knowledge all the time. If they did, experts would quickly become overwhelmed. What is important about these developments are the principles and possibilities they demonstrate.

But what is most remarkable is that these developments are deeply *integrative*. Learning, assessment, technology, collaboration across students, teachers, communities, business partnerships are all tightly interwoven. Technology makes a wide range of information more immediately accessible. To make learning innovative and integrative, teachers no longer have to work endless hours preparing integrated curriculum units. Teachers can concentrate more on stimulating and supporting the learning process. Moreover, when learning is more collaborative and increases the amount of interaction and learning among students themselves, students who are still trying to catch up in their second language and students from a range of cultural minorities perform much better, because they make sense of and talk through what they are learning with other classmates (Cummins, in press).

In these most recent efforts to transform teaching and learning, social and intellectual capital are not at odds, technology and humanity are not pitted against each other, assessment and teaching are not working at cross purposes, and diversity and the public good are achievable together.

Sadly, the central tendencies of most government reform strategies do not reflect these purposes of learning. Too much change is foisted on teachers that has little chance of promoting the cognitive and social transformation that Lucas and others are talking about. Tax cuts, structural alterations, new forms of governance, league tables of performance, standardized tests, and market-oriented window-dressing have precious little to do with improving teaching and learning in the way we have described. It is time we had a new kind of accountability in education – one that gets back to the moral basics of caring, serving, empowering and learning. Whenever anyone concerned with education wants to do anything with a curriculum, a school, or a school system, they should be called to account for how their actions and proposals will improve or at the very least, not damage teaching and learning.

The second pillar of learning is the realization that it is impossible to accomplish the deep purposes of student learning unless teachers are continuous learners themselves. For children to become better learners, teachers must learn how to become better learners too – not as a one-shot solution to particular crises, but as an ongoing professional obligation. Teachers have a right to high-quality professional learning experiences and opportunities. They also have a responsibility always to be on the look-out for ways to teach and reach their students more effectively. Teachers who see teaching as something that is mastered in early career and that they then know how to do for the rest of their life, get poorer results than teachers who see teaching as being intrinsically difficult, in which improvement is always possible and necessary, especially in a culturally diverse and technologically complex society. Students become good learners when they are in the classes of teachers who are good learners. Professional learning should therefore not be seen by teachers, schools, governments or communities as peripheral to teachers' priorities. Time invested in teachers' learning, if integrated with the development of a collaborative culture, is time that ultimately pays off for students' learning. Teachers, more than anyone, are essential to the creation of a better learning society. They can scarcely do this well if they are not good learners themselves.

In complex, rapidly changing times, if you don't get better as a teacher over time, you don't merely stay the same. You get worse (Stoll & Fink, 1996). Professional learning can therefore no longer be an optional luxury for course-going individuals, nor a set of add-on workshops to implement government priorities. Professional learning must be made integral to the task of teaching, with time for it built in by the system and ongoing commitment to it regarded as a basic professional obligation of teachers themselves. Only then will teachers be able to deal effectively with the numerous new challenges they face and to get better in their job over time.

The current situation in teaching is somewhat analogous to a lawyer who spends all of his or her time in the courtroom, and little time 'preparing the case'. Teachers have little daily time outside 'the courtroom' and what they have is often not closely related to preparing their case. It is time dedicated to meetings, workshops and courses that are often disconnected from the refinements needed to improve their own teaching on an ongoing basis. The teaching profession is badly in need of transformation so that there is a closer functional relationship between ongoing preparation of the case and their own professional learning.

The third pillar of learning is that which takes place between schools and their communities. If schools were good learning organizations, they would constantly search for ideas, input and information about how to improve their practice and get better results over time. Long-lived companies are organizations that have learned how to work together internally, and that have developed new skills and attitudes as a result of learning interactively with their changing environments. This long term success research shows, "is based on learning" (de Gues, 1997:20).

Many school staffs are getting better at learning how to learn from each other as colleagues. But in very many cases, schools are unable or unwilling to learn from parents. In her research on parent-teacher relationships, Vincent (1996) concludes that the relationship most teachers prefer to have with parents is one where parents support or learn about what teachers already do. Parents are expected to back-up the teacher by undertaking practical tasks in the classroom, or signing home-school contracts in relation to their own children, for example. Enlisting this kind of parental support leaves the teachers' existing professional authority intact. What teachers seem less inclined to do is put themselves in positions where they are the ones who learn from the parents.

Teachers don't usually want to wash their dirty linen in front of parents. They prefer to set their own directions and solve their own problems as professionals first, then inform the parents later. They normally enlist parental support in enforcing discipline policies rather than ask parents what kind of discipline policy they want in the first place. And, as we are seeing in secondary schools involved with us in a school improvement project, where schools have parent survey data that indicates areas of dissatisfaction with the school, teachers prefer to interpret such data as showing their failure to get their message across properly ("what we're doing is fine, but we're obviously not communicating it well"), rather than recognizing that the parents might have a point!

Some teachers who are self-assured with students are anxious or arrogant when working with parents. In the next chapter, we will look at why teachers find these relationships so difficult. The point we want to emphasize here is that parent-teacher relationships dominated by fear, anxiety and control must be transformed into ones characterized by shared commitment and reciprocal learning – where teachers learn from parents as well as vice versa. When teachers make learning a moral priority in their relationships with parents, they get helpful feedback on their practice, they value the diverse perspectives and expertise that everyone brings to a problem, they include parents who are so often seen as part of the problem, in devising necessary solutions to it, and they "own" problems with parents instead of getting drawn into mutual recrimination about who is to blame for them.

To love, to serve, to empower and to learn – when these four aspects of moral purpose are seen as central ends of education, and when they underpin not just what students do but what teachers and parents do as well, then relationships between schools and the world beyond have real moral depth to them. Take these moral purposes away and the edifice of educational change and of connecting with what's "out there", collapses into faddism and opportunism.

Passion and Emotion

Teaching is a passionate vocation.

Pursuing moral purpose in complex times is an emotional roller coaster. Choosing demanding purposes and sticking with them in difficult times, draws on every ounce of emotion teachers have. The pleasures and rewards to be gained from this kind of emotional engagement as a teacher are immense, but the risks of exhaustion and disillusionment when purposes are dashed, or people can't live up to them, are equally great. We have already looked at the part teachers play in developing their students' emotional intelligence. Going deeper also means understanding the emotional nature of teaching itself, and how different kinds of change strategies, working environments and relationships with the world beyond school impact upon it. The theory and practice of educational change need to probe deeper into the heart of what teaching is and into what moves teachers to do their work well.

Movement is the key idea here. Emotions are basically "mental states accompanied by intense feeling . . . [which involve] bodily changes of a widespread character" (Koestler, 1967:226). The Latin origin of emotion is *emovere*: to move out, to stir up. When people are emotional, they are moved by their feelings. They can be moved to tears, overcome by joy, or fall into despair, for example. Emotions are dynamic parts of ourselves, and whether they are positive or negative, all organizations, especially schools, are full of them.

New research and insights on the role of emotions are destroying popular assumptions that emotions cloud logic. Damasio (1994) observes that "an important [and erroneous] aspect of the rationalist conception is that to obtain the best results, emotions must be *kept out*. Rational processing must be unencumbered by passion." Emotions, says Damasio, are actually indispensable to rational decision-making. People who are emotionally flat might be able to perform abstract intellectual tasks, but they can't make practical judgements of human value:

> *In real life, a purely logical search through all possibilities is not possible (because of limitations of resources, multiple goals, and problems of coordination with others). Nevertheless, we must act . . . despite our limitations we must take responsibility for our actions, and suffer their effects. This is why emotions or something like them are necessary to bridge across the unexpected and the unknown, to guide reason, and to give priorities among multiple goals.*

> (Oatley & Jenkins, 1996:123)

In today's turbulent and complex environments, we operate with multiple goals and imperfect knowledge. We can't be perfectly rational by pinning down and choosing between all the possible ends and conceivable means for reaching them. Emotions help us narrow and judge among the range of possibilities. In healthy individuals, emotions don't distort rationality, they enhance it!

Teaching, of course, is charged with emotion – positively and negatively. It is a passionate vocation. Good teachers are not just well-oiled machines. Computers can never replace them. They are emotional, passionate beings who fill their work and their classes with pleasure, creativity, challenge and joy. Good teachers are passionate about their ideas and field of knowledge; about social issues, locally and worldwide; and about the children and youth they seek to inspire. Being passionate does not mean blindly loving all students – some are hard to love on given days. But passionate and caring teachers are more likely to set the right course, to stay with it when the going gets rough, and to avoid a "permanent fog of fatigue, ritual, routine or resignation" (Fried, 1995:19). They are more likely to go deeper.

The innovation-oriented Grade 7 and 8 teachers we identified earlier, drew on a broad repertoire of strategies to try and reach their students, get them motivated, help them understand. They changed their teaching so it meshed with what their students wanted, used support strategies that raised the comfort level of students with learning difficulties, tried "to involve the kids as much as possible – find out their interests", took pride when their special education students "shone", used portfolios to discover what children found "fun" so this could be incorporated into teaching them, made the class-room "a safe place where people can be free to express their ideas" and feel comfortable interrupting or asking questions, encouraged students to share their feelings, played soft background music if it helped children perform better in tests, and used humour, lots and lots of it, as a "great equalizer; it breaks the tension and the stress."

Throughout all these strategies, teachers were actively engaged. A second language teacher said, "you have to be prepared to dance and stand on your head and do just about anything to get kids to respond and participate." Teaching methods are one of the great rhetorical battlegrounds of educational reform. Teacher-centredness is pitted against child-centredness; individualized and small group-based instruction is set against whole class teaching. Our teachers scuppered these stereotypes. They learned and embraced an array of methods. Teachers were vivid and vital presences in their classes who facilitated learning extensively but sometimes taught directly and inspirationally as well. Teachers who are no more than coaches or guides-by-the-side risk emptying teaching of its passion.

Teachers in our study felt it was important to be yourself as a teacher, and to let your own emotions and feelings show through from time to time. As Farson (1996) says, "it is indeed in moments when we *lose* control rather than exert it, that our humanity as leaders shines through – by sharing our joy, excitement, disappointment, and sometimes even our outrage too." Vocalizing outrage requires great personal courage. There are times when it is important to speak up passionately about what's wrong in our schools and in government policies that affect them.

Teaching is also charged with negative emotion. Oatley (1992) describes how negative emotion is usually precipitated by two factors. First are threats to people's sense of self. When the boundaries of the self are breached, and its inadequacies are exposed, this results in shame, embarrassment, humiliation or anger. Second, are threats to people's goals and purposes. People may be obstructed from achieving their goals; compelled to realize other people's goals and agendas that they find inappropriate or repugnant; pursuing standards or goals that are beyond their reach; or unable to choose between multiple goals. All these things lead to anxiety, frustration, anger and guilt. Negative emotion, that is, comes about because of threats to identity and to achieving one's goals. Conversely, positive emotions usually occur under opposing conditions – when identity is secure and desired goals are being achieved. Understanding that negative emotions are connected to issues of purpose and identity poses questions about the management (or mismanagement) of educational change and its impact on teachers.

Among these emotional impacts on teachers are: frustration and guilt where caring and conscientious teachers work themselves to the point of burnout; shame and humiliation where teachers are made to feel exposed and vulnerable in front of others (e.g. by insensitive inspection processes or being "shamed" as a failing school); and stress and anxiety when multiple innovations and endless change make it impossible to feel competent, and ultimately lead to depletion of energy and loss of hope.

The long term consequences of negative emotions are well documented. Prolonged stress is bad for your immune system, your mental health, your capacity to care for yourself and others, and can even be fatal. Individual stress management and personal wellness programmes may be helpful as responses to these difficulties – but only up to a point. It is self-defeating to try and make individuals emotionally healthy when their organizations remain fundamentally sick. This is why we later advocate relationship-building and partnerships as one way of dealing with emotional vulnerability. Isolation, we will argue, is the enemy of emotional health.

> *Studies done over two decades involving more than 37,000 people show that social isolation – the sense that you have nobody with whom you can share your private feelings, have close contact – doubles the chances of sickness or death.*

(Goleman, 1995:226)

Passionate teachers need interaction with, and support from others to avoid becoming exhausted. All teachers need to inspire each other through collaborative work, to take advantage of the power of emotional resources, and to provide the interpersonal safety nets when the going gets rough. There is no reason why this support cannot also come from people who are not teachers as well.

However, this is precisely the problem. Emotions are virtually absent from the literature and advocacy of educational change in areas like strategic planning, cognitive leadership, problem-solving, or standards-based reform. Even the idea of organizational learning which is on the very cutting edge of change theory is almost exclusively cerebral in its emphasis. Teachers need to take more care of their own emotions, colleagues (with community members) need to take more care of each other; and educational policymakers could do with developing more emotional intelligence of their own – especially when it comes to empathizing with what teachers have to do in the face of educational change.

Teaching is hard emotional labour, often pleasurable but always taxing, even in the best of times. Working yourself up to feel positive, hopeful and enthusiastic with your students, even when you don't immediately feel like it, is always difficult. When you are exhausted by external and constantly shifting change demands, disheartened by endless public criticism, feeling guilty that you haven't improved enough, and forever in fear of being labeled a failure, then the emotional labour of teaching can become almost impossible to bear. It is then that teachers become exhausted, disheartened and cynical – with negative effects on their teaching and students that spiral continually downwards.

Going deeper into the emotions of teaching and educational change should therefore mean understanding how to create collaborative workplaces for teachers that promote positive, even passionate emotional relationships to teaching, learning and improvement. Equally it means avoiding damaging this positive emotional engagement by not overloading teachers, not distracting them too far from their classroom rewards and purposes, and not consistently interfering with or interrupting the emotional "flow" of their relationships with students and colleagues by constantly inspecting, testing, evaluating and having them account on paper for everything they do.

Keeping the flames of passion alive in teaching is a challenge for all teachers, especially as their energy levels subside and as they have to suffer the slings and arrows of people outside their classroom who see their job very differently. It is also a responsibility of all those who work with teachers and affect their lives – to inspire the love of learning, to keep the heart in teaching, and to make their own partnerships with teachers emotionally enriching ones. Our next chapter focuses on what it means for teachers to work with others outside the school in emotionally enriching and morally purposeful ways.

Hope

It is easy to be hopeful when things are rosy. It is essential to be hopeful when they are not.

More than anything else, more than expectations, passionate engagement or standards, teaching is about hope. Every child is one teacher's hope for the future. The bigger the child's problem, the greater the teacher's hope. Hope matters most for those children who least seem to warrant it. The best definition of hope is 'unwarranted optimism'. There is no advantage to being hopeful when the conditions warrant it. Hope's real value is when the conditions are not hopeful. Hope should never disappear.

Earlier, we showed how hope is linked with feelings of self-efficacy – the self-fulfilling belief that you really can make a difference in people's lives. Hope is the ultimate virtue on which a decent and successful school system depends. Yet, as Cszikzentmihalyi (1990:7) observes, "frustration is deeply woven into the fabric of life." This is especially true for teachers. The more they care, the more anxious they get. The more they emotionally detach themselves, the poorer decisions they make. Hope can extricate people from this paradox. Having hope needn't mean leaving everything optimistically to fate. In its most positive and practical manifestations, hope means more than having a naive, sunny view of life. Hope makes a difference when it represents the capacity not to panic in difficult situations, the belief that all is not lost, that problems can be solved and that one's own actions and interventions can have an important effect.

> *From the perspective of emotional intelligence, having hope means that one will not give in to overwhelming anxiety, a defeatist attitude, or depression in the face of difficult challenges or setbacks. Indeed, people who are hopeful evidence less depression than others as they maneuver through life in pursuit of their goals, are less anxious in general, and have fewer emotional distresses.*

> (Goleman, 1995:87)

Whereas prolonged stress undermines the immune system, hope or optimism can actually lead to better health. People who are optimistic and hopeful *are* more resourceful and healthier. They do better under difficult circumstances. Not only do they avoid the costs of perennial pessimism, but they also *gain* the benefits of hopefulness.

Hope can be found in the most improbable places, and its effects can be personally transformative. Cszikzentmihalyi (1990:196-7) cites a research study where in-depth interviews were conducted of homeless "street people". Predictably, the researchers found many people who had given up hope or turned to drugs, violence and crime. But many others seemed able to create satisfying, even enriching experiences from their seemingly impoverished condition. In their study of resilient higher risk children who 'overcome the odds', Werner and Smith (1992) found that the most salient turning points on the road to recovery for troubled individuals were being supported by someone who cared for them, and entering a positive relationship with an accepting partner. The road from vulnerability to resilience was marked by "the number of sources of help that the teenager attracted, including support from teachers and peers as well as from family members" (p. 200).

Traditionally, hope, along with faith and charity, were relatively passive virtues. When hope is linked with moral purpose and emotional engagement, it can become an active, dynamic, transformative force. Hopeful teachers, in this sense, are not naive, nor are they complacent. They empathize with, but do not accept and capitulate to situations which do not meet their own standards of moral purpose. In Saul's (1995:165) words, they "refuse to mind their own business".

All is lost if teachers succumb to pessimism and cynicism. Cszikzentmihalyi (1996: 19-20) interviewed the Canadian novelist Robertson Davies who said it best:

> *Pessimism is a very easy way out when you're considering what life really is because pessimism is a short view of life. If you look at what is happening around us today and what has happened since you were born you can't help but feel that life is a terrible complexity of problems*

and elusiveness of one sort or another. . . It is very much easier to be tragic than it is to be comic. I have known people to embrace the tragic view of life, and it is a cop-out. They simply feel rotten about everything, and that is terribly easy.

(Cszikzentmihalyi, 1996:19-20)

Similarly, Paulo Freire (1982) said that one of the most basic conditions necessary for 'true dialogue" to occur is hope: "dialogue cannot be carried out in a climate of hopelessness. If the dialoguers expect nothing to come of their efforts, their encounters will be empty, sterile, bureaucratic and tedious" (p. 80). When cynicism and despair are all around us, when things sometimes seem so manifestly hopeless, educators and those who work with them need to draw deeply on their reserves of active hope. It is during these times that it is critical to keep on struggling for virtuous causes even when they seem lost; to continue believing that one's own efforts really can make a difference; to seek out fellow travellers to work with who can help fulfill hopes together; to confront, or by-pass authority figures who are lacking in imagination and are inclined to be obstructive; to not take 'No' for an answer; to see that the glass may be half full instead of half empty; and to look for opportunities in reform demands that are thrown their way instead of dwelling only on the problems. It is easy to be hopeful when things are rosy. It is essential to be hopeful when things are not.

Urging teachers to stay hopeful even under negative conditions might be construed as encouraging political quiescence. Putting the onus for change on the shoulders of relatively powerless individuals, can be seen as excusing and drawing attention away from the morally questionable acts of powerful groups and individuals. These latter groups are often the very ones most responsible for making other people's lives so difficult and for creating cultures of hopelessness. But we needn't and shouldn't choose between individual change and institutional change. Nor should we choose between personal transformation and political transformation. Focusing on either dimension, in isolation, is folly. Expecting individuals to change without offering any institutional support is politically manipulative and dishonest. Similarly, expecting institutions to make all the change without individuals making any commitments themselves, creates long-term dependency. Such an orientation fosters complacency when things go well and hopelessness when they don't.

It is not only possible, but also essential to build connections between hopefulness and the structural conditions that promote it. Hopeful change agents are painfully aware that the current working conditions of teachers militate against positive and successful reform. The development of collaborative work cultures among teachers and with communities requires different and more supportive internal structural conditions as well as very different external relationships. Accomplishing this will also require pushing for, expecting and demanding those who make new policy frameworks to alter the incentives and structural conditions that currently frustrate reform.

In a world where the Cold War has ended, a black leader now rose to rule South Africa, and a seven year old former street girl can find two tins of beans in her kitchen cupboard for someone more hungry than herself, it is important to hang on to and pursue our hopes in education, and to create the conditions in which hopefulness can bloom. In the next chapter, we "go wider" beyond the school to outline how moral purpose, emotional engagement and active hopefulness can be furthered by building strong alliances between people within schools and partners outside them, and how these alliances and partnerships are strongest and most productive when they are morally grounded, emotionally rich and infused with hope themselves. Hope does not travel alone.

Chapter 3
GOING WIDER

The health of an organization is closely related to the health of its environment: in attending to its environment, an organization is attending to itself.

(Binney & Williams, 1995)

Reframing Relationships to the Outside

In Chapter 1, we showed how and why the world outside school is intruding more and more into teachers' work within it – to the point where what's inside the school and what's "out there" beyond it are increasingly indistinguishable from each other. It is vital, we said, that schools don't try to ignore these outside forces, for if they are unprepared, they will only fall prey to their most damaging effects. Engaging with what's "out there" is therefore essential. The question is – how can schools do this best?

We have warned against making connections that are superficial or merely expedient. Contracts and committees are popular policy solutions to the problems of getting schools to connect with their wider environments. These approaches, on their own, have limited and sometimes negative effects. Good connections are complex, not simple; they take time to build rather than being initiated at the stroke of a pen; and they rest on a deep understanding of what educational purposes the connections will serve.

It is going to be very difficult to open up organizations such as public schools. First, like many organizations in the past, public schools have largely evolved by keeping the outside world at bay. They have accumulated all kinds of structural and cultural habits of keeping people out. In Kanter's words "leaders of the past often erected walls. Now they must destroy these walls and replace them with bridges." (1996: 91)

Second, this process of bridge-building will be extremely demanding because it will require cooperation among people who have not been used to working together, indeed among people who have a lot of legitimate reasons to mistrust each other. Somehow these barriers of suspicion and mistrust must be superseded.

You will not find us romanticizing about alliances and partnerships which produce smooth-running, mutually supportive love-ins of people cooperating for the common good. Going wider – when the stakes are high, when previous relationships are non-existent or negative, and when the differences are greater than the similarities – is a messy, frustrating, conflict-ridden, and time consuming business. It can also be an immensely satisfying, and rewarding one. In other words, it is change at its worst and at its best.

Third, the best opportunities for building positive connections are not always obvious. Excellent partnerships can grow from inauspicious beginnings. The secret of building strong partnerships is persevering beyond initial awkwardness and lack of trust to try and understand each others' viewpoints, develop a common focus and create "win-win" relationships. Going wider means developing and sorting out beneficial alliances with people and groups outside the school, even when you don't always initially know how they will turn out. It means trusting processes as well as people.

Thus, positive relationships with the world outside school are not at all straightforward. On the one hand, they require educators to capture the commitment and imagination of individuals and groups "out there" to join in supporting the purposes and passion of education we described earlier. On the other hand, they require openness of mind and generosity of spirit towards these external groups (though this doesn't mean blithe or blind acceptance of everything they demand). Sometimes, the priority will be repelling intruders whose policies and demands divert us from or do harm to the core mission of education. In their study of over 800 schools, Newmann & Wehlage (1995) found that schools which did best in increasing student achievement were collaborative internally, but were also heavily involved in and influenced by external frameworks and expectations: "external agencies helped schools to focus on student learning" (p. 4).

Connecting to the outside will rarely mean easy consensus. It is a struggle that can take many forms. We will describe four of these – formal relationships, community, partnerships and alliances, and networks. Central to all of them, though more to the last three, is the idea of collaboration.

Collaboration is a process of shared creation: two or more individuals with complementary skills interacting to create a shared understanding that none had previously possessed or could have come to on their own.

(Schrage, 1990: 40)

Relationships of *formal association* are necessary in complex societies where most people no longer live in small villages with taken for granted commitments and loyalties to each other. These relationships are chosen rather than traditionally presumed, rational more than emotional, and they connect people through the specific tasks or roles they perform for each other, rather than as whole persons. They are most evident in market relationships and commercial transactions, in the official business of bureaucratic organizations and procedures, in modern government and in the groups we call professions (sometimes known as professional *associations*). Despite the benefits, impersonal relationships of association now consume too much of our lives and our time. Market relationships have reduced many of our choices to clinical self-interest. Bureaucracies have become rigid and faceless. Professions have too often shrouded themselves in mystification, distancing themselves from their clients, and turning into what Adam Smith called "conspiracies against the people".

In connecting with what's "out there", formal relationships such as those of school councils, school choice and professional self-regulation only get you so far. Deeper, stronger more informal connections are what's needed most.

Communities are made up of face-to-face relationships of people who live or work in the same place (community of place), are committed to a common faith or values (community of mind), and feel a sense of belonging and obligation to each other (community of friendship) (Sergiovanni, 1994).

They are emotional relationships as well as rational ones and they deal with people "in the round", not just in terms of their specific tasks and roles. As Henry (1996:18) says in her study of relationships between schools and parents in poor neighbourhoods, "authentic casual contact or informal relations between parents and educators may be more important than formalized events."

Parents need to feel that the school is a *community of place* for them. The school must be posted with welcoming signs, not warnings. The office must be clearly visible and accessible. Parents should feel welcome in the staffrooms and/or have a space of their own to gather together. They must not be made to feel that classrooms are off-limits to them. And the school facilities should be open to the neighbourhood out of school hours, and sometimes within school time as well.

Communities of friendship with parents are built through informal contacts, social events, being welcomed as volunteers in classrooms, through lots of interaction about the work their children take back and forth between home and school, through two-way report cards, by being contacted when their children have done well (and not just when they've been a problem), and by contacting teachers themselves to show appreciation to them, and not just find fault.

Schools should also develop *communities of mind* with their parents. Do parents feel they are listened to properly and that their views are taken seriously? Are relationships with parents treated as ones that teachers can learn from, and not just relationships of one-way communication? Do teachers try to avoid conflict with dissenting parents and "blind them with science and mystification," or do they discuss problems together (really listening to what parents have to say as they do so)? Creating a community of mind means acknowledging differences, wanting to learn from them, and working for closer agreement. This is one of the biggest obstacles that schools have yet to overcome.

A third way of connecting with what's "out there" is through partner-ships and alliances. Partnerships are more specific than communities. They involve people from different groups coming together to explore and share common or complementary skills and interests, that are to their mutual benefit.

Goodlad (1994) has been a tireless advocate (and practitioner) of a new "powerfully productive symbiosis" between schools and external agencies, which, he argues, depend on:

1. *distinctive differences between the courting parties;*

2. *the complementarity of these differences -the degree to which each side contributes to the other's lack;*

3. *the extent to which the courting parties first envision and then comprehend through experience how much this complementarity depends on fully shared commitment and effort;* and

4. *the powerful contextual needs or demands such as societal priority or available resources.*

(Goodlad, 1994: 103-104)

Successful partnerships are a two-way street where all parties realize they have something to learn. Finding partners and building alliances is a good way to share resources – as airlines and other businesses are discovering. Partnerships also strengthen people's capacity to learn and get better over time by opening them up to divergent viewpoints and honest feedback.

Educationally defensible partnerships must have a clear moral purpose. In terms of our themes in Chapter 2, they must demonstrate how they will help improve teaching, learning and caring. They must put service to students' education before the self-interest of boosting corporate image, or increasing people's profile in the community. They must be actively committed to social justice by agitating for changes that favour all students, not just the highest achieving or most privileged ones who promise the biggest success and corporate return. And they must be genuinely reciprocal so that partners are open to learning from and being influenced by each other.

The last way of connecting with the external environment is through networks. Lieberman & Grolnick (1997:193) studied 17 professional development and educational improvement networks in the United States, and described them as follows:

> *Networks engage school-based educators in directing their own learning, allowing them to sidestep the limitations of institutional roles, hierarchies and geographic locations, while encouraging them to collaborate with a broad variety of people: socially, ethnically, institutionally, and so forth.*

Networking provides teachers and others with a way to share ideas, swap experiences, exchange lesson plans, provide support and undertake professional learning based on their perceptions of their own needs and agendas, and not on mandates imposed by others. Networks put a high premium on members' own knowledge – though most also connect with expertise from the outside. They work best when they have a clear interest or compelling idea around which people can cluster.

Teacher networks have existed for many years in different parts of the world, but their power is really being boosted by computer technology. This enables teachers to interact with each other, about things that matter most to them, day or night, at the touch of a keyboard.

All four forms of connecting with the environment are important. None are mutually exclusive. But governments and administrators too often believe that formal management committees and market choice will do the trick! They could not be more wrong. Without investing in the other three kinds of connection, their policy measures are destined to have little or no educational success.

Five Key External Forces

The best way to deal with what's "out there" is to move toward the danger.

The power of community, alliances and networks can be best seen in relation to five of the most prominent external forces, namely:

1. parents and communities;

2. government policy (using assessment as the example);

3. technology;

4. businesses; *and*

5. the changing teaching profession (including teacher education and unions).

In all these areas, our one major compelling message is that, paradoxically, the best way to deal with what's "out there" is to move towards the danger. Fight is better than flight; engagement more effective than avoidance. Moving towards external 'dangers' with purpose, passion and the power of collaboration and alliances is the essence of what's worth fighting for out there.

1. PARENTS AND COMMUNITIES

Treating relationships with parents and communities as powerful learning relationships is essential.

Nowhere is the two-way street of learning more in disrepair and in need of social reconstruction than the relationship among parents, communities, and their schools. Teachers and principals need to reach out to parents and communities even, and especially, when the initial conditions do not support such efforts. Henry's (1996) study of parent-school collaboration in poor neighbourhoods concluded:

> Educators have to go out into their communities with empathy, and interact meaningfully with their constituents. Being professional can no longer mean remaining isolated in the school (p. 132).

This will involve shifts in power and influence. But it is not power in and of itself that counts. It is what new power arrangements can accomplish that matters:

> To seek power is to raise and begin to answer the question: to seek power to change what? Changing the forces of power in no way guarantees that anything else will change . . . To seek power without asking the "what" question is not only to beg the question but to avoid, and therefore to collude in cosmetic changes.

(Sarason, 1995: 53)

The "what" question is: "What will it take to mobilize more people and resources in the service of educating all students?" The research is abundantly clear about the answer. Teachers cannot do it alone. Parents and other community members are crucial and largely untapped resources who have (or can be helped to have) assets and expertise that are essential to the partnership. However well or badly they do it, parents are their children's very first educators. They have knowledge of their children that is not available to anyone else. They have a vested and committed interest in their children's success, and they also have valuable knowledge and skills to contribute that spring from their special interests, hobbies, occupations and place in the community.

At the same time, we have said that too many parents are seriously disengaged from their own children's lives and learning. Parents need staff development as much as teachers do.

We also know that neighbourhoods and communities make a difference. Quality of parenting and neighbourhood support can be enhanced in any socioeconomic class, and it results in students performing better in school and getting into less trouble (Steinberg, 1996).

Further, we showed earlier that investment in early childhood education is crucial. In their international review of "Combatting School Failure", the Organization for Economic Cooperation and Development, OECD (1997) found that a solid system of early childhood education is one of the most consistent preventors of later school failure (and all the costs of dealing with it as a society). Ontario's Royal Commission on Learning (1994:12) stated it this way:

> *Good research has increasingly demonstrated that long before any child arrives at school, much learning has already taken place; just ask any parent. But the nature of that learning varies greatly; just ask any teacher. The kids who enter our schools for the first time often arrive from vastly different worlds of experience – worlds that profoundly affect their ability to learn in both positive and negative ways.*

Early childhood education is a powerful antidote to these inequities. We are the first to agree that healthy societies make healthy schools. But it is not in the moral or self- interest of teachers to wait for "society" to respond. They can begin by making partnering with parents and the community a priority. They can join the wider society that is influencing them instead of trying to keep their distance from it. Epstein (1995) identifies six types of school and parent/community involvement which in combination improve student learning and adult engagement with their children's education:

- parenting skills (improving home environments);

- communication (two-way between school and home);

- volunteering or adult aides (recruiting and organizing adult help);

- learning at home (specific home tutoring assistance);

- decision-making (involving parents and developing parent leaders); *and*

- coordinating community agencies (identify and develop communit service).

Note that schools councils (the fifth item) and community coordination (the sixth) represent only two of six forms of involvement, and not the most important ones at that. They are relationships of "association" with all the limitations we have mentioned. For the same reason that site-based management (involving teachers) bears no necessary relationship to changes in the culture and learning of the whole school, school councils and coordination procedures *per se* do not necessarily affect student learning. And why should they? The establishment of a council involving a handful of parents (not to mention matters of representation and skill) could not possibly improve the learning of hundreds of students in the school. The formal procedures of committees are also intimidating to many parents who do not work in white-collar jobs and have often done badly in school themselves. Failure to attend meetings does not mean unwillingness to support one's children or the school – though educators may often see it that way. Instead, the biggest difference is achieved through building strong informal relationships, being willing to share power that benefits students and committing to learn from each other.

What, in practical terms, does this mean? Just some of the possibilities of treating relationships with parents and the community as learning relationships include:

- school reports, written in plain language, that encourage and leave space for parents to respond. What's at stake here is not simplifying what students learn, but how we describe what they learn.

- three-way parents' night interviews, involving parents, students and teachers together. One of the teachers in the Grade 7 & 8 project, describes its benefits in these words:

One of the most positive things that has come out of these interviews is that the parents sit down for two to three hours and listen to their child. Parents meet one another for the first time. You've got, say, four kids, who are from four different areas of the world, and their parents are sitting there talking about the kid who is making the presentation.

(Earl & LeMahieu, 1997)

- carefully disaggregating marks so that the criteria and evidence behind assessment judgements are open, accessible and clear.

- surveying parents' attitudes to school issues (e.g., discipline or new technologies). However, it's important that teachers don't control all the communication by designing the questions and analyzing the results by themselves. Parents should be involved in the survey process.

- engaging parents and communities with the uncertainties of upcoming change. When facing change, schools usually work out their internal professional response first, then inform the community later through meetings or newsletters. Yet, counterintuitively, (as we have seen in our own school improvement work) when schools involve communities *with* them in the uncertainties of change at the outset, support and understanding are much more likely to be forthcoming.

- setting up focus groups of parents when changes are pending (or to decide what changes might need to be pending). One strategy used in places as far apart as Manchester, England (Beresford, 1996) and Manitoba, Canada (with the Gordon Foundation's secondary school improvement project), is to get focus groups of parents to talk about what they want for their children's education and how well the school is providing it while teachers listen.

Treating relationships with parents and communities as powerful learning relationships is essential. In many cases teacher education programs do not prepare their graduates to work effectively in these ways. Moreover, dealing with what's "out there" is clearly stressful. Yet schools must move towards this uncomfortable world as Dolan (1994) so clearly captures:

> In a school, where mistrust between the community and the administration is the major issue, you might begin to deal with it by making sure that parents were present at every major event, every meeting, every challenge. Within the discomfort of that presence, the learning and the healing could begin.
>
> (Dolan, 1994: 60)

There is no avoiding the discomfort of diversity if things are going to improve.

2. GOVERNMENTS

Schools and districts can take the lead. . . by establishing data-based procedures and information that link to their teaching and to what students are learning.

Unfortunately, governments spend most of their time focussing on changes in structure and procedure – governance, finance, formal requirements. As we said before, these kinds of changes only get you so far in connecting with what's "out there". The road to hell is paved with reform strategies that attempt to extract compliance from reluctant and alienated implementors. Success is built with people, not pieces.

Linda Darling-Hammond (1992) puts it this way:

Two very different theories of school reform are working in parallel and sometimes at cross-purposes. . . One theory focuses on tightening the controls; more courses, more tests, more directive curriculum, more standards enforced by more rewards, and more sanctions. These reformers would improve education by developing more tests and tying funds to schools' test scores. . . A second theory attends more to the qualifications and capacities of teachers and to developing schools through changes in teacher education, licencing, and certification processes,. . . professional development schools, efforts to decentralize school decision making while infusing knowledge, changing local assessment practices, and developing networks among teachers and schools (p. 22).

Having external assessments and internal development of teacher capabilities are not mutually exclusive as we have argued. Too often compliance concerns completely overshadow capacity-building which focusses on the motivation, skill and resources that are needed to perform at a high level. Effective educational change always needs a blend of pressure and support, but most governments have exerted far too much pressure (which suits short-term political time-frames) and provided not nearly enough long-term capacity-building and support.

In Chapter 4, we will set out some guidelines for governments. Here we look at the other side of the coin. How should teachers and principals connect with governments, even and especially when they appear to act so unreasonably? Assessment and accountability policies are a good case in point. Many people argue that making accountability procedures explicit and visible will increase student achievement. The assumption is that test scores and performance indicators will nail teachers (and students) down to meeting agreed or imposed expectations and standards. But it's not clear, in this theory, how teachers will then decipher and use this information to improve their teaching and help their students do better.

Realistically, though, assessment data will often still be used to judge schools and teachers in ways that provide little motivation or leverage to know how to make corresponding improvements. The temptation under these circumstances is to close the door and ignore the assessment demands as far as possible. Paradoxically, however, it's important that teachers and principals move towards the danger. How can they do this?

First, some of the most unreasonable government policies can be successfully resisted by teachers as a whole. In England in the early 1990s, for example, teachers who were weighed down with interminable government testing requirements and immense overloads of curriculum content, rose up together and refused to implement the tests – leading to a commission of inquiry (The Dearing Report) that cut back on the curriculum and streamlined the tests so they were workable.

Second, schools and districts can take the lead on these issues by establishing data-based procedures and information that link to their teaching and to what students are learning. In this way data drive teachers' own improvement efforts. When teachers do this, outside demands for data and accountability from central office or inspection bodies are no longer experienced as extraneous and overwhelming demands. Because data compilation is an ongoing part of their work, responding to accountability requests requires little or no additional effort from them.

Third, teachers can take more initiative in communicating their results to the public. Crude public (especially media) presentations of school-by-school test and examination results in league tables that take no account of the kinds of student population each school serves, are damaging and humiliating to the worst performing schools, and provoke understandable anger and denial among their teachers. But instead of just contesting the validity of test results and how the media interpret them, teachers need to show what they are doing to increase academic performance, and they need to capture the public imagination by compiling more rounded portrayals of their school's performance and achievement – demonstrating how far they are adding value to student's levels of achievement over time, putting scores in context, adding extra information about success in sports, the arts, community service, etc. All this is easier to do, of course, if teachers already compile and interpret their own assessment data on a continuous basis.

In assessment, as elsewhere, the overall lesson is that teachers need to become highly skilled and knowledgeable in those very areas where they feel most vulnerable to government and media attacks. In other words, what's worth fighting for in assessment policy is to learn to become less vulnerable to its inevitable intrusion by becoming more proficient in dealing with the instructional and political complexities of student achievement information, and more effective in contesting misuses of data and advocating students' interests. This is another compelling reason for going wider.

3. TECHNOLOGY

Ensuring that technological change will really benefit student learning depends on its being driven by its critics as much as its most ardent advocates.

There is no better example of how what's "out there" is already right "in here" within the school itself than the ubiquitous presence of technology. Computer technologies can break down the barriers of schooling enabling students and teachers to participate in virtual learning communities across the world, where there is instant access to almost limitless information and where physical space is no longer a limit to learning. Some of the most ardent advocates of computers in education are the corporate creators of the new technologies themselves (e.g., Gates, 1995). New technologies are seen as having intrinsic value, as being desirable and inevitable, as requiring teachers to make best use of them, and as deserving maximum possible resources to be dedicated to them. Many people regard new technologies as a great gift to education. The only problems they foresee are ones of technical development and human implementation (Bigum & Kenway, in press). New technologies are viewed as the indispensable educational tools of the twenty-first century. Some even see them as portending the end of institutionalized education in schools and classrooms as we know them – with teachers turned into coaches, guides or facilitators. A totally wired world of learning without walls is the utopian dream of the most ardent technophiles. In a cartoon referred to in the Ontario Royal Commission on Learning's Report (1995) one student announces to his friend: "I'm only going to school until it becomes available on CD-ROM."

Critics are much more skeptical about the educational benefits of the new information and communication technologies. They point out that all technological innovations giveth and they also taketh away! Automobiles, for example, brought people independence and mobility, but they also led to accidents, laziness and pollution (Postman, 1992). Some critics believe computers destroy printed literature and face-to-face conversation. Emotionally inspired creative writing generated by teachers with passion, imagination and a rich vocabulary, may be eclipsed by electronically assisted writing that concentrates on technically adequate communications alone. Text writing in point-and-click formats may lack the richness of dramatic narrative forms more common in books. Stoll (1995) is perhaps the most articulate and vitriolic proponent of this position:

> *Computer networks isolate us from one another rather than bring us together. We need only to deal with one side of an individual over the*

net. And if we don't like what we see, we just pull the plug, or flame them. There's no need to tolerate the imperfections of real people . . . we lose the ability to enter into spontaneous interaction with real people . . . All of us want children to experience warmth, human interaction, the thrill of discovery, and solid grounding in essentials: reading, getting along with others, training in civic values . . . Only a teacher, live in the classroom can bring about this inspiration. This can't happen over a speaker, a television or a computer screen (p. 58).

Proponents and critics both have a point. In most cases, the truth is usually somewhere in between. But this truth doesn't happen by itself. It is something that teachers must create and fight for even harder. It's time we moved beyond the false dichotomy that we must choose between machines and people. New technology will insinuate itself into more and more aspects of our lives. The challenge for teachers is to turn this inevitable intrusion into a powerful tool for learning. Technology need not and will not do teachers out of a job. Educationally, it makes them *indispensable*!

The sheer volume of information that technology spews out exposes any weaknesses or deficits in pedagogical design concerning how this tool can best be used. In the absence of well prepared, critical and caring teachers, computer technology can result in an information glut where much of the information students get is superficial and indiscriminately arranged. It can lead to students designing cute covers for their work more than thinking deeply about the intellectual content and substance of it. And it can isolate students from each other.

By contrast, educators equipped with a clear and sophisticated approach to teaching and learning, can use technology to deepen, extend and invigorate students' learning. When George Lucas set out to capture what makes learning exciting, he found teachers and students immersed in the use of interactive technology, working together on cooperative inquiry and problem-solving, and producing products and learning outcomes of the most exceptional quality:

Technology is . . . giving educators the power to offer more experimental learning – the kind of learning that has taught all of us most of what we know. Schools have become hamstrung in proving hands-on learning, aside from sports for example, by the limitations of resources and the logistics of taking students off-site. Through realistic simulations of real-world environments, jobs, and problems, students are able to have rich and rewarding learning experiences. They are traveling to distant parts of the world via the World Wide Web, investigating ocean bottoms, and learning to fly airplanes without leaving the classroom.

(Lucas, 1997: 211)

His examples show how technology is being used to deepen students' understanding of what they are learning. They describe, for instance, how "assistive technologies" can give students with disabilities the chance to participate in learning in ways never before possible. Analyzing data, editing texts, overcoming disabilities in motor-skills, creating graphic and written products of professional standard, conquering the geographical barrier to communication, accessing experts, learning by simulation, accessing quality information and learning to critique its sources and biases (e.g., by comparing "raw" Reuters news-releases with the spins that popular and quality newspapers put on them) – are just some of the immense benefits computers can bring to the classroom.

However, left to its own device, the technology juggernaut serves only the needs of commerce and the market. It's a tool so why would it have purpose, passion and hope? Why would it be concerned about equity?

Unless we find a way for poor children to have access, outside the school, to information technology equipment (linked to a network), it is quite likely they will eventually fall behind. The possibility of creating a new class of technological illiterates, with disproportionate privileges, is only too real.

(Ontario Royal Commission on Learning, 1995: 11)

By far the biggest weaknesses in how schools use new technologies are pedagogical and strategic. Levin and Riffel (1997) studied how school and system administrators in five school districts responded to external changes, including computer technology. Their conclusions carry profound messages for how (and how not) to introduce new technologies into schools. In most cases new technologies are not yet resulting in deeper dialogue about teaching and learning. Levin and Riffel found that among all the possible uses of computers, only 54% of administrators felt they would help people to see student-teacher relationships in different ways.

> *Technology can transform the work of people, but often doesn't. . . It is often used first to do old tasks; it takes time to discover new possibilities. . . (yet) there are significant barriers to inquiry-oriented instruction in schools — traditional models of teaching and learning are deeply embedded in the structure and culture of schools. (p. 113)*

There is no avoiding the central issue. Even with new technologies, no significant changes will occur for students unless we have more and better discussions about how to transform and improve teaching and learning in our schools so that students develop deep understanding and can apply what they know to new situations. The biggest weakness of technology is the absence of sophisticated instructional designs required to take advantage of the available information. Developments in cognitive science, we showed earlier, are creating new pedagogical possibilities in what it means to teach and learn for deep understanding, and to apply what we know to new situations. This makes teachers indispensable. They must become the pedagogical experts of the future, where their values and know-how counterbalance the inane uses of computers arising from the commercial imperative of technology-as-machine.

Not all excellent teaching depends on new technologies. Computer advocates must avoid making those teachers who have been breaking new ground in other ways in their classrooms for years, feel that their efforts are not being recognized or valued. Moreover, there will always be a place for inspired presentation alongside skilled facilitation.

Finally, as we have said elsewhere, we must learn from "resistance". Levin and Riffel (1997: 109) observe:

> *Teachers who have not embraced technology were termed 'resisters'. . . and described by 90 percent of. . . respondents as in need of substantial retraining. There was no mention of their views, little appreciation that their concerns might turn out to be constructive in the long run.*

If we are serious about the moral purposes of empowering and learning from colleagues, then resistance to technology should be treated with respect, as a source of insight and not as a sign of awkwardness and deficiency. Ensuring that technological change will really benefit student learning depends on it being driven by its critics as much as its most ardent advocates.

4. BUSINESSES

Teachers with moral purpose, critical judgement and the skills of teamwork are best positioned to take advantage of the corporate resources "out there".

If teachers' relationships with parents create complications for their senses of professionalism, their relationships with the business community raise even greater technical and political controversies. Is business a supportive partner or a self-seeking pariah? Should teachers embrace the idea of establishing closer links with corporations or should they defend education against enterprise culture? Developing and taking a moral and practical stand in relation to these immensely controversial issues is one of the greatest challenges for teachers and their professionalism today.

In reality, relationships between schools and the business world are already expanding. These take many different forms such as business investment in new technologies within education, business support for new vocational initiatives, co-operative education (work experience) programmes for students, the use of visiting speakers from the corporate world in schools, schemes for teachers to have placements in industry (including shadowing people in industry to understand the skills the working world requires), business-sponsored development of curriculum materials, and broader sponsorship of general educational activities.

Supporters of stronger partnerships between education and the working world point to the need for schools to develop skills, knowledge and capacities more suited to the working demands of the information age. They also acknowledge, pragmatically, that when government expenditure for public education is in shorter supply, schools must seek potential sources of funding and investment elsewhere. Critics contend that business is actually a major cause of the educational problems for which it claims to be offering solutions. They argue that business exploits its educational influence to treat schools as markets, students as captive consumers, and the curriculum as a place to peddle business values. While some critics advise educators to steer clear of the business world altogether, others acknowledge that business influences are here to stay and recommend that teachers and principals adopt a position of responsible marketing towards them (Kenway et al., 1995). Figuring out what kinds of corporate connections are most beneficial for the school (and for society as a whole) is one of the new responsibilities of the schools today.

Using moral purpose as the guiding framework for partnership, the school seeking or courting a business partner should ask these questions.

- Will it put service to students before company self-interest?

- Will it serve the interest of *all* students, or the most needy students, and not just the favoured few?

- Will it be genuinely reciprocal, so that schools will have things to teach business as well as vice versa?

- Is the company socially responsible in what it produces, in the environmental impact of its production, and in the treatment of its own workforce and their families?

- What impact will this partnership have on other schools in the wider web of market relations?

A creative change agent will seek out business and other partners who can benefit and support their student's learning. A truly moral and courageous one will turn aside the chance of investment if the wrong strings are attached to it.

Already many corporations have raised their philanthropic activities and profile, and have explicitly taken on social responsibilities beyond their own profit-making. More business leaders also realize that a healthy society is good for business. "More educators and employers" says the Lucas report "are realizing how intimately their interests are intertwined" (Lucas Foundation, 1997: 142).

The report of a major study by OECD, (1994) concludes that business partnerships can be useful for expanding teachers' knowledge of the modern workplace in business and industry. Teachers, in turn, can use these insights to design a more work-relevant curriculum. For example, teachers are sometimes surprised to learn just how much the intellectual requirements in the workplace have risen and how important critical thinking and communications skills are to employers.

Similarly, businesses have something to learn from schools. The more that schools become learning organizations the more they will have to offer businesses. For example, in one elementary school, its corporate partner – a motor manufacturer – was so impressed with the school's collaborative ways of working, it invited the principal and her staff to train their own executives! After all, learning is the business that schools are in, and all organizations are striving to become better learners in the knowledge society.

In sum, there are many reasons why educators should be wary of business connections, but committed partnerships between schools and the corporate community can also yield remarkable benefits. The benefits and the dangers exist together. Teachers with moral purpose, critical judgement and the skills of teamwork are best positioned to take advantage of the corporate resources "out there".

5. The Changing Teaching Profession

Teaching as a profession has not yet come of age.

If you look closely, the biggest revolution we are talking about when we urge schools to get "out there" more is *changing the teaching profession.* To go deeper and wider in the ways we are advocating means that the teaching profession cannot stay the same. If you examine the underlying message of even the most supportive government commissions on teaching, you are compelled to conclude that teaching as a profession has not yet come of age. It needs reform in recruitment, selection, status and reward, redesign of initial teacher education and induction into the profession, continuous professional development, standards and incentives for professional work, and (most important of all, perhaps) in the day to day working conditions of teachers. Yet there appears to be little political will to launch sustained reforms in teacher development and in the organization of the teaching profession more widely.

As teachers work more and more with people beyond their own schools, a whole gamut of new skills, relationships and orientations are fundamentally changing the essence of their professionalism. This new professionalism is collaborative, not autonomous; open rather than closed; outward-looking rather than insular; and authoritative but not controlling.

More than anything, the new professionalism makes huge demands on teachers' own learning – learning how to keep modifying and extending their teaching as research discovers more and more about children's learning styles, multiple intelligences and ways of understanding; learning how to integrate new technologies into their classrooms; and learning how to interact effectively with adults "out there" to deepen their understandings of and get more support for the students they teach. Some of this learning will need to be undertaken in preservice teacher education, when teachers first learn to teach. But in a complex environment, where demands change relentlessly, and teachers may work for 30 or 40 years beyond their preservice training, the learning can't stop there. Nor can the learning be packaged up in brief workshops and structured courses.

Teachers today and tomorrow need to do much more learning on the job, or in parallel with it – where they can constantly test out, refine and get feedback on the improvements they make. They need access to other colleagues to get this learning from them. Schools are poorly designed for integrating learning and teaching on the job. The teaching profession must become a better learning profession – not just incidentally, at teachers' own individual initiative, but also in the very way the job is designed.

Ways must be found for educators to step out into wider learning networks; for schools and universities to form partnerships in which teacher education and school improvement are pursued in tandem; and for government and union leaders to go beyond the dance of despair that often ends up demoralizing the best of our teachers.

In *What's Worth Fighting For? Working Together for Your School* we showed that the quality of teachers' relationships with students in the classroom is closely affected by the quality of relationships that teachers have with each other outside the classroom. We made the case for teachers developing stronger collaborative work cultures or professional communities with their colleagues in their own schools. We stand by this. Teachers today must learn to become leaders of their colleagues as well as teachers of their classes. However, good colleagueship need no longer be confined to professional relationships within teachers' own schools. One thing that is "out there" for teachers is abundant expertise, insight, learning and support from educators elsewhere in the system. At a time of rapid change and increasing professional expectations, getting access to this professional learning and expertise is more important than ever.

There are plenty of opportunities to join electronic learning networks, and innovative program projects. We, ourselves, have been heavily engaged in school-district university partnerships in which initial teacher education, ongoing professional development and school improvement are integrated. These partnerships extend far beyond small clusters of professional development schools (which leave the wider systems that preservice teachers will enter later unchanged), to relationships that try to transform these broader systems themselves. In turn, schools of education soon realize that their cultures must also change if the partnership is to work. Across the world, there are more and more opportunities available for joining or creating consortia of this kind. In these partnerships, cohorts of student teachers, teams of university and school faculty, and sets of partner schools are going through powerful learning together. They are, in short, *reculturing* the profession.

It is hard to see how teaching can become a more vigorous learning profession unless teachers together take (and are allowed to take) more control over their own learning agenda. Otherwise, professional development degenerates into one-shot workshops on the latest government or district policy. It is fundamentally in the interests of teachers and those they teach that teaching becomes 'A Self-Regulating Profession'. Teachers must have and endeavour to meet an exacting set of professional standards of practice. Although there is increasing support across the world for this, these standards are often viewed as things that other people or agencies set for teachers. We are more likely to raise standards of teaching if we expect that teachers work on this themselves. This means that the teaching profession must be largely self-regulating. This self-regulation must not be merely symbolic or bureaucratic. It must get to the heart of and stay close to what good quality teaching and learning is about. And it must involve other partners – so they can have input into the standards and give them public credibility.

A self-regulating body with a majority of elected teachers (but including wider community representation of other legitimate stakeholders in education) is best placed to set, maintain and constantly look for ways to raise its own collective standards of practice. Such a body can act as a powerful and independent pressure group on government to create policies that promote the high standards of practice and professional learning which teachers have set themselves. This approach to self-regulation gives teachers the privilege and responsibility of establishing their own collective professionalism, so they are in the vanguard rather than being the victims of educational reform.

It is ironic and frustrating that, in different parts of the world, whenever teacher unions have proposed a self-regulating body, governments have blocked it; and wherever governments have taken the initiative, teachers have opposed it. The only thing worse than blind trust is blind mistrust! It's time for governments and unions to put old enmities aside and struggle together with greater openness and generosity for the higher moral purposes and standards that professional self-regulation can achieve.

None of this will happen unless governments end their obsessions with criticizing and controlling their teachers, and invest more in capacity building instead. Nor will it happen unless a new teacher unionism can flourish in which union leaders argue and act as passionately for their own positive visions of teaching, learning and change as they do for business-as-usual defences of pay, class sizes and working conditions. Though still a minority, more and more local, state and national union leaders are taking the risks of leading the profession in these new and visionary directions.

If teachers are to put some sanity into standards and get the learning they need to meet those standards (as well as responding to the challenges of an ever more demanding environment), they have to connect more deeply and regularly with the wider profession. At the same time, at every level, they must see themselves as change agents of that profession.

Moving Forward

In diverse, complex and turbulent times, partnerships, networks and community-building with people beyond the school are vital for improving the quality of learning within it. But not any kind of partnership will do. Partnerships are of little benefit to students or teachers if they are superficial, cynically opportunistic, or bogged down in bureaucracy. Good educational partnerships are sound in purpose, steeped in mutual learning, and full of passion.

Building successful partnerships and using them to benefit student learning, we have shown, requires a different and dynamic kind of professionalism where teachers work with partners both outside and inside the school in ways that are open and authoritative, emotional as well as rational, and in relationships of reciprocity and equality.

We don't deny that stepping out represents great personal and professional risks for educators. But it is better to move toward the danger, contesting and reconfiguring the terrain with purpose and passion. It's also better to do this with other people – finding and creating allies in obvious and not so obvious places. These people will help you not only to survive, but also to realize your hopes and attain your goals.

Chapter 4
GETTING OUT THERE

Lost causes are the only things worth fighting for.

Mr. Smith Goes to Washington

Guidelines For Action

What's Worth Fighting For Out There? is for those who want to tackle the most important but seemingly intractable educational problems of our time. It is about fighting for lost causes and being persistent in your efforts even when others around you seem to have lost all hope. How does one go about confronting a challenge of such massive proportions? The guidelines for action in this chapter show what going deeper and wider really means. They involve educators and the public moving towards each other, instead of shrinking away from differences, or attempting to overpower each other. The following pages contain action ideas for teachers, principals, governments and parents, indeed for anyone who wants to do something to establish education as a vital force for individual and societal development. Most of all this chapter involves exercising hope as a political, moral, and active virtue.

Education happens when hope exceeds expectation. Teaching is what makes the difference. Teachers everywhere work miracles without many of the resources or supports they really need. Without hope, teaching is nothing. It stops being a mission and becomes just another job. Too many of our teachers are starting to lose hope. We are in serious danger of undermining a fundamental truth of educational effectiveness – that the learning and emotional lives of students are profoundly dependent on the learning and emotional lives of teachers.

Low morale, depressed, feeling unfairly blamed for the ills of society? You must be a teacher.

(Times Educational supplement, 1997)

An editorial accompanying this quote in the English *Times Educational Supplement* (January 10, 1997) notes that "the nation's leaders claim to put [education] at the top of the agenda, but they leave teachers at the bottom". Yet, it is precisely in times of great instability and societal transformation, when teaching and learning need to become ever-more powerful, that a positively engaged teaching force is essential. Those who work in and with our schools need to experience a stronger spirit of hope. More than this, and remembering that hope is an *active* virtue, they need to build a clear *strategy* of hope as well. Being hopeful, remember, is not about being passive. It involves the use of power – practising positive politics to achieve deep reform. Hope is rooted in the confidence that the direction one is taking makes sense, even if the obstacles seem insurmountable. There are three vital components of such a strategy of hope and we start with these three general guidelines for action:

1. capture the public imagination;
2. focus on relationships; *and*
3. beat the path of change as you walk it.

1. CAPTURE THE PUBLIC IMAGINATION.

It is the responsibility of all of us to move this agenda forward. None of us should wait for others to take the lead, but we should always invite them to join in. Breaking the log-jam and building a strategy of hope depends on a new unionism in which teacher leaders advocate and commit to innovative reforms for the common good; on governments who are prepared to help transform the teaching profession in positive ways; on university leaders fashioning new partnerships with public schools; on a media that celebrates teaching and learning and doesn't just denigrate them; on businesses, labour and community organizations working together to build stronger capacity for improvement in schools and on countless individual parents, teachers and citizens sharing greater generosity of spirit towards each another, as they work through the discomfort of their differences for the benefit of the next generation.

Capturing the public imagination emphasizes an outward orientation. It involves developing a more seamless relationship with local communities. It also requires a more proactive and open relationship with local and national media. Take the risk of inviting media to write stories about what your school is doing. Be available and open to requests from the media. Try to be open and non-defensive when real problems are discussed. Analyze media stories about your school, your district or education in general. Be hard-nosed about inaccurate attacks by immediately correcting falsehoods through direct contact and counter articles to the editor. Take the high road, but be relentless about getting people's attention when education is portrayed in a misleading way.

It's hard enough for teachers to collaborate with each other. It's harder still for them to work effectively with people outside the school whose views of how learning and teaching should be, often seem so fundamentally at odds with theirs. Yet, it's exactly here that a strategy of hope must begin.

Rational disagreement, however brilliant, hardly ever shifts the viewpoint of government. It makes little sense to argue your way into extinction, even when you know you're right. Instead, teachers must win the hearts and minds of parents, communities and the public – the constituencies on whom governments ultimately depend. Teachers must show practically and concretely how difficult and important teaching is today, how different it is from the teaching that the public remembers from their own school days, how and why teaching needs to improve even further, and what kind of support teachers will need to secure that improvement. The public must know what new learning skills students need, and how new teaching methods are necessary to deepen students' understanding and their ability to use knowledge. Teaching for understanding must be made publicly and palpably clear. This is the first part of a three pronged strategy of hope – to capture the public imagination.

2.   FOCUS ON RELATIONSHIPS.

Those who imagine strategies of legislation and prescription will really work are treading a fine line between ignorance and arrogance.

The second prong is to build hope not so much by meetings, newsletters, or other formal mechanisms, but by focussing on relationships. Farson (1996: 91) says that what "people suffer most in their lives (is) from failed or failing relationships . . . or from lack of relationships – isolation, alienation, erosion of community".

Any educational reform strategy that improves relationships has a chance of succeeding; any strategy that does not is doomed to fail. This is why formal policies and procedures themselves will never provide the answer. Decades of research on and experience in human relations and organizational development in the business world, have shown that good relationships aren't just emotionally more fulfilling. They also lead to higher productivity, improved problem-solving and better learning. One of the most thorough long term studies of company failure and success concludes that, "companies die because their managers focus on the economic activity of producing goods and services, and they forget that their organizations' true nature is that of a community of humans" (de Gues, 1997: 3). In examining numerous social programmes from the perspective of how to 'spread what works', Schorr (1997) concludes that it was replicating relationship-building that accounted for success, not just the transfer of an idea or product.

If relationship-building is central to success, why is this basic principle of change violated so often? Because it is easier to pass legislation, announce a policy, prescribe new standards, and reorganize. Those who imagine strategies of legislation and prescription will really work are treading a fine line between ignorance and arrogance. It is much harder to work through complex problems with diverse personalities and competing groups. Yet altering relationships for the better is absolutely necessary for successful reform.

3.   BEAT THE PATH OF CHANGE AS YOU WALK IT.

The third prong of a strategy of hope is to be both resolute and flexible in building relationships with people outside the school. What's "out there" is now "in here". Growth and sheer survival will require beating multiple new paths of change with others outside your classroom and your school. Trying more than one option, never giving up, improving and adjusting as you go are essential if your hopes are to have a chance of being fulfilled and sustained.

De Gues calls the line by poet Machado – life is a path that you beat while you walk it – "the most profound lesson on planning and strategy that I have ever learned". De Gues (1997: 155) reflects that

> *When you look back, you see a clear path that brought you here. But you created that path yourself. Ahead, there is only uncharted wilderness. . . In the final analysis, it is the walking that beats the path. It is not the path that makes the walk.*

What's Worth Fighting For Out There? is ultimately about committing to working with people you may once have mistrusted or feared, building positive relationships with them, improving and adjusting these relationships as you go, and never letting up in the quest. It is about getting out there and seeing your work from other people's point of view. It is about drawing on inner reserves of hopefulness and continually seeking to build networks of support and action to make those hopes come true. It is about beating a path of learning and moral goodness.

Guidelines for Teachers

The best ways to get "out there" are integral to learning itself.

Each and every teacher can get "out there" in ways that will make a difference for their own and other teachers' students. This needn't mean more work, additional duties, or diversion from the classroom. The best ways to get "out there" are integral to learning itself. They involve students or are about what students do. All teachers are already leaders of children. Every teacher can also be a leader of colleagues and in their school's community. The following guidelines can be used by all teachers, from the beginning teacher who walks in the door for the first time, to the experienced veteran who has the chance to leave a lasting legacy:

1. Make students your prime partners;

2. Respond to parents' needs and desires as if they were your own;

3. Become more assessment literate;

4. Refuse to mind your own business;

5. Develop and use your emotional intelligence; *and*

6. Help to recreate your profession.

1.   MAKE STUDENTS YOUR PRIME PARTNERS.

Recently, we spoke to five hundred school administrators in Western Canada. We were introduced by a special announcer. Confidently, he approached the platform from the back of the room, carrying a small metal box. Placing the box behind the lectern, he stood on it, and faced his audience. Our announcer was Jacob, a Grade 4 student. He delivered one of the most technically accomplished introductions we have heard. Without looking at his notes, with no hesitation, pausing in all the right places and maintaining perfect eye contact throughout, he listed our names and titles, professorships and scholarships, books and papers with absolute aplomb. The applause he received was thunderous – a very hard act to follow!

Jacob is part of a programme called *Astounding Announcers* – his class chose the title. The class makes over 60 introductions and announcements a year to parents, Chambers of Commerce, professional and community groups. Becoming an *Astounding Announcer* requires a lot of learning, practice, and sheer hard work. We asked Jacob's teacher what led her to create the programme. There were two reasons, she said. First was her own passion for learning – she had completed a public speaking course that was so inspiring and empowering for her, she wanted to pass on the educational benefits to her own students. Second, was the mounting governmental, media and corporate criticism of public education. *Astounding Announcers* gave her a way to get "out there" with her students and present passionate, imaginative and practical examples of what students and teachers were achieving these days. One class influencing the educational views of over 60 groups a year – quite an impact! This single example embodies many of the principles we outline in this chapter. It involves moving toward the public and capturing its imagination.

Getting "out there" in other words, doesn't and shouldn't mean abandoning your students. The most important points of connection between home and school are students themselves. Every piece of paper they carry, story they tell, or secret they hide speaks volumes about their teachers and their experience in school. Teachers who are approachable to students have more chance of being approachable to their parents. After more than 800 interviews with English secondary school students, Rudduck, et al, found that according to students, the teachers most likely to increase their commitment to learning were the ones who:

- enjoy teaching the subject;
- enjoy teaching students;
- make lessons interesting and link them to life outside school;
- will have a laugh but know how to keep order;
- are fair;
- are easy for students to talk to;
- don't shout;
- don't go on about things (e.g. how much better an older brother or sister was);
- explain things and go through things students don't understand without making them feel small; *and*
- don't give up on students.

(Rudduck, et al, 1997: 86)

93

Students responded to teachers whose classrooms were filled with positive emotion (enjoyment, humour, approachability, and empathy), and full of hope (not giving up). Yet we saw earlier that too many secondary students in particular find that it is just this sense of care and connection that is missing from relationships with their teachers. This is a disturbing void.

In *Overcoming the Odds*, Werner and Smith (1992) found that it was sources of emotional support with caring adults, peers and others that rescued high risk children from being doomed to a life of failure and grief. The Manitoba School Improvement Program funded by the Gordon Foundation is another case in point (MSIP, 1997). For eight years this programme has been supporting grassroots teachers to change how they work with students and fellow teachers. Students who once seemed sullen and unreachable often became the most ardent advocates for positive change once the right connection had been made. One student spoke about how "what seemed to be an impossible path to walk in life, has been altered" thanks to teachers who had worked with her. "But what I am most thankful for is that all of you have exposed me to an atmosphere of hope and strength".

Good relationships are the foundation of worthwhile learning. All teachers, including secondary school subject teachers, should attend to their students' emotional intelligence as well as other aspects of achievement. Care should be the responsibility of every teacher, not just those in departments or centres of guidance. So our first guideline recommends that you try and form a bond with each and every student you teach, and make relationships with the home a vital part of this bond.

One secondary school with which we are working caters for large numbers of special needs students from all across the city. Organizing community meetings and parental involvement is a nightmare. One teacher suggested that every teacher make just five positive calls to parents a week, about how their son or daughter is progressing – reaffirming for the student and involving the home. Can you and your colleagues make this kind of commitment yourselves?

Making students your prime partners also means putting them and their learning at the core of all other partnerships you build – and involving them directly in the process. One of the best ways for you and your colleagues to improve your skills in new technologies, for example, is to ask your students to help train you – they often know much more about it than you do, and will learn important teaching and leadership skills in the process. When working with corporations, let them look at classroom learning, invite them to judge science fairs and inventors' festivals; ask individual students to approach them for advice with projects and investigations, etc. And with parent partnerships, devise ways for students and family members to engage in learning or talk about learning together through discussing portfolios, three-way interviews, or undertaking homework assignments (e.g., kitchen science experiments) that you have constructed for them to work and reflect on together.

In times of reform, everybody claims they have the students' interests at heart. Rarely are students consulted directly themselves. Rudduck and her colleagues note that "we do not regularly and automatically discuss (possible changes) with our students and allow their reflections to help shape our policy for change". But, they continue, when students have been consulted, people have found that . . .

> *young people are observant, are often capable of analytic and constructive comment, and usually respond well to the serious responsibility of helping identify aspects of schooling that strengthen or get in the way of their learning.*

(Rudduck, et al, 1997: 75-76)

Involve students in their own learning, in the partnerships you build with people outside school, and in how you manage educational change. Making students your first partners is the prime directive in building all other partnerships with people "out there" beyond the school.

2. RESPOND TO PARENTS' NEEDS AND DESIRES AS IF THEY WERE YOUR OWN.

Be authoritative about your expertise, but open about your uncertainties.

Teachers experience more anxiety about their relationships with parents than almost any other aspects of their work. Realistically, to the teacher, one student is one among many. To the students' parents, he or she is their most treasured possession. You are seen to be the gatekeeper of the child's future, and parents are prone to feel they are losing control over their child's destiny. The worse the future looks or the bigger the economic downturn, the more concerned they are likely to become. This is an explosive mixture. How should you deal with it?

First, try and see things from their point of view. In her study of teachers who are also parents, Sikes (1997) found that becoming a parent changed how many teachers treated the children in their own classes. They saw their students through new eyes. As one teacher commented, when you become a parent, everyone's child is your child and your child is everyone's child. Education becomes more serious (it matters even more, now), and also more relaxed (you realize that children can't be expected to be perfect all the time).

Second, if you can't intuitively grasp the parent's perspective by being a parent yourself, try to learn it. Talk with parents informally in the school and community. Ask for reactions to newsletters, report cards and homework assignments. Survey their opinions. Really listen to what they have to say. This is especially important when parents are culturally different from you; when you are a teacher of "other peoples' children." Join a community organization, locally or otherwise, that gets you in touch with other citizens.

Third, put your anxieties into perspective; 90% - 95% of your interactions with parents are probably satisfactory or better. But do you tend to dwell on the 5% or so that went badly – that were awkward or argumentative? Don't let these exceptions colour how you approach parents in the future. Keep things in perspective.

Fourth, don't let your only meaningful communication with parents be on parents' night. If this is the only chance parents get to discuss their child's progress, it will push the anxiety levels too high. Build trust, don't presume it. Develop strong relationships with parents and other partners and they are less likely to devour you. It's hard for people to eat something they've had a relationship with! Interact with parents in multiple ways through things like portfolios, school social events, even casual conversation at the school gates. This will lower the intensity levels on the other occasions when you have to meet more formally.

Fifth, be influenced by parents. Parents have a different kind of wisdom about their children, which can complement professional knowledge. The power to teach does not, of course, rest solely in the classroom. As we argued in chapter 3, new reciprocity with parents and the community is central to *What's Worth Fighting For Out There?*

Last, you will still come across parents from time to time who are angry or argumentative about how you are treating their children. How can you minimize these occasions and respond to them when they do arise? Most importantly, remember that anger is often a consequence or by-product of other emotions that people feel (Oatley, 1992). So try to get past parents' anger and the defences you are inclined to erect against it, to discover what deeper emotions and issues are at stake. This is a test of your own emotional maturity and intelligence.

Perhaps parents are frustrated that their educational plans and purposes (which may be different from yours) are not being heard or acknowledged as valid and important. Perhaps parents feel guilty that they don't spend enough time with their children, ashamed that they can't seem to control them or afraid that their children will be kept back a year or will fail. Find ways to connect with parents, empathize with their feelings and deal with what's behind them. Find authentically positive things to say about their child, but don't shrink from honest criticism either. Be yourself. Be authoritative about your expertise, but open about your uncertainties. Show you're not perfect as a teacher or a parent. Tell stories about yourself, in this regard –

it will make you seem less defensive and give you a way to connect. Make parents part of the solution not part of the problem by striving to respond to parents' needs and desires as if they were your own.

3.   BECOME MORE ASSESSMENT LITERATE.

Teachers who have nothing more than their own individual intuition to fall back on when they face parents, easily feel exposed, vulnerable and threatened. Assessment issues make teachers feel especially insecure. These feelings of insecurity can be dispelled if teachers agree on assessment criteria based on discussions and decisions about samples of student work that they look at together. Once teachers have developed some shared confidence about their assessment judgements, they are likely to feel more self-assured (and paradoxically more open) when discussing any particular assessment decision with individual parents. In the absence of this kind of "assessment literacy", teachers feel, and are vulnerable.

In Chapter 3, we described how teachers can expand their assessment repertoires, show parents and students how they have arrived at their assessment decisions, collect assessment data as an ongoing part of classroom learning (perhaps entering scores and comments into a computer data base rather than markbook), monitor how well their students are achieving over time and communicate the results clearly to parents and the public. There are three points to add here.

First, wherever possible it is important to integrate your assessment practices into your learning and when you can, to make it a form of learning in itself (e.g., self-assessment, peer assessment, portfolios). Clear and detailed assessments that go home regularly with students also provide learning for parents. Parents attach exaggerated importance to grades and percentages when they have nothing else to fall back on – when they have little or no idea what work their child has been doing and what it is worth. In the absence of current information, they clamour for something that makes sense and seems familiar – the marking and grading systems of their own school days. Incorporating assessment data into a cascade of student work that goes home regularly for parents to see, erodes these stereotypes with the daily reassurance of rich information.

Second, becoming more assessment literate also means acting as critical consumers, and engaging with assessment and other research data that might be relevant to your school. Interpreting league tables of performance, mediating research findings, understanding how achievement scores should be understood in relation to the community each school serves – this is all technically difficult work. There should therefore be one teacher leader in each school who is responsible for engaging with the outside world in terms of research, assessment and accountability, and for helping teachers and parents interpret the results.

Third, remember that effective schools are ones in which principals and teachers focus on student learning outcomes and link this information to improvements in teaching and learning strategies. They are in a much better position to 'move towards the danger' when they have clear data to present to the public. They know and can demonstrate what they are talking about. Taking control of your own data means taking charge of how the argument about standards and accountability is conducted.

4.   Refuse to Mind Your Own Business.

Saul (1995) and others have said that we can no longer depend on institutions to do the right thing, and that concerned individuals are an untapped source of reform. Real individualism, he says, is the obligation to act as a citizen. As citizens who refuse to mind their own business, teachers must not act as if their business is only in the classroom, and must realize that what happens outside the classroom can profoundly affect their work for better or worse. Most obviously, refusing to mind your own business means taking political action against wrong-headed reforms that railroad teachers through change at an unworkable speed, or that put forward changes which will damage public education. While we should always be wary about 'getting better at a bad game', teachers with purpose and passion must protest damaging government action, not because they are in despair, but precisely because they are hopeful and actively determined to make things better for their students.

Refusing to mind your own business isn't just about making protests against governments, though. It should also be an act of individual moral courage that leads you to question colleagues or parents whenever you see them do harm to students. In her research on teachers' ethical dilemmas, Campbell (1996) has found that teachers are extremely reluctant to intervene in this way. Yet, it is important to express moral outrage towards colleagues when warranted, as much as towards abstract governments. More than this, refusing to mind your own business means getting outside of your classroom to create collaborative cultures among teachers where teachers support one another but also hold each other accountable by reviewing their curriculum, assessments and teaching strategies together.

In the permeable schools and volatile reform contexts of today, refusing to mind your own business is another way of saying you should redefine the business you are in to encompass the key external forces that can help you succeed or prevent you from doing so.

5.   DEVELOP AND USE YOUR EMOTIONAL INTELLIGENCE.

> *An especially essential aspect of emotional intelligence on which good teachers rely is empathy.*

Getting "out there" and refusing to mind your own business is emotionally challenging. As Goleman (1995) says, "in the day-to-day world no intelligence is more important than the interpersonal" (p. 42). There are two ways in which individuals can work on their emotional intelligence; one they can do privately, the other in groups.

Individuals can use the checklist in Goleman's (1995: 283-284) five domains of emotional intelligence to become more aware of their own strengths and weaknesses with respect to 'knowing one's emotions', 'managing emotions', 'motivating oneself', 'empathy', and 'interpersonal effectiveness'. Goleman (1995: 180) also describes a technique that reduced stress levels dramatically in individuals. The method is remarkably simple. Write for fifteen to twenty minutes about the most traumatic experience of your life, or about some pressing worry of the moment. Teachers could write once a week about the most upsetting or uplifting moment of the week. What they write can be kept private. Similarly, in individual terms, when the going gets rough, teachers can step back and focus on a higher purpose, take a longer time perspective, or remind themselves that hope is healthy irrespective of its predictive power.

Group support involving one or more partners is also crucial. While solitude has its reflective healing powers, feeling absolutely alone with a problem is destructive. Collaborative work cultures, like healthy families, can provide emotional safety nets and other supports to help us through difficult periods.

An especially essential aspect of emotional intelligence on which good teachers rely is empathy. In any occupation, it is important to step outside yourself, to see your work from another angle and to understand other people's point of view. One of the most important ways to get "out there" and develop your powers of empathy is to shadow a student through their school day from time to time and experience what learning (or failing to learn!) looks like from the other side of the desk. Exchanging classes with teachers at a very different grade level, joining one of the many projects to spend time in the business community, or really taking the time to listen to parents' concerns when they talk to you, will all improve your ability to empathize with the many adults "out there" whom your work increasingly includes.

Emotional intelligence is not a matter of hiding or containing emotions, but of channeling or focussing them. Groups consisting of members with purpose, passion and alliances with others "out there" can be far more politically efficacious when they draw on their collective emotions and clarity of resolve in each situation they face.

Finally, we need to appreciate the fact that not only are both reason and emotion involved in effective decisions, they are interactive. Listen to gut feelings. Take cues from intuition. Feelings and intuition should not automatically guide our action any more than logic should, but they should garner the same respect. Reconciling the respective powers of emotion and cognition increases one's individual and collective capacity for positive change.

6. HELP TO RECREATE YOUR PROFESSION.

The next few years, we believe, will be a defining era for the teaching profession.

The teaching profession, we have said, has not yet come of age. Attaining maturity is a great struggle. Even until the mid 1960s, teaching was seen as demanding but not technically difficult. You prepared for class, taught it and marked papers afterwards. It didn't take long to learn to teach and once you'd prepared for it, you knew how to do it for the rest of your career. You relied on experience and intuition to do it well. Outdated as this image of teaching is today, it is still widespread and influential among the wider public. This is the kind of teaching they remember when they were in school. If teaching is not all that difficult, why not cut back on teachers' resources, levels of support and time away from the classroom? Everybody else has cut back – perhaps teachers should take their turn as well!

This pervasive myth and the damage it does to public support for education is one of the most compelling reasons for breaking down the walls of schooling, and for communicating and creating new visions of professionalism that are in tune with the complex realities of schools today – one where it is essential for teachers to work in teams with each other in open partnership with parents, employers, universities and others, to benefit the diverse range of students they teach.

When many governments seem intent on deprofessionalizing teachers, putting them on temporary contracts, restricting their time to work with colleagues, relentlessly criticizing their work, and reducing their areas of autonomy and discretion over teaching and curriculum decisions, garnering public support that is in tune with the complexities of the job is imperative. For that to happen, the image and the reality of professionalism in teaching need to change dramatically.

The next few years, we believe, will be a defining era for the teaching profession. Will it become a stronger learning profession? Will it become a force for societal change and social justice? Can it develop its own visions of and commitments to educational and social change, instead of simply vetoing and reacting to the change agendas of others. The potential is certainly there. Numerous projects and partnerships such as the four with which we have been most associated – The Learning Consortium and the Peel Partnership in Ontario, the Manitoba School Improvement Project, and the Building Infrastructures initiative in four American urban school districts – have produced scores of grassroots leaders among teachers and administrators who are beginning to think and act like change agents, questioning tradition and the status quo and taking risks under adverse circumstances. These hidden, unsung heroes and many others in change projects and networks around the world are working against the grain. There are many more of them than most of us realize. But these initiatives on the ground have rarely gelled into a collective professional vision where teacher unions and other professional organizations take the lead, spearhead change and improvement initiatives of their own, and carry their members with them. What can you do to help recreate your own profession as a leader of educational change and not just a reactor to other people's change agendas?

First, you can support the idea of professional self-regulation, electing people to self-regulating bodies who have the vision and commitment to raising the standards and the public image of your profession, developing powerful approaches to and expectations for professional learning, and bringing about changes that really benefit students. Self-regulating professional bodies in teaching should not be allowed to ossify into the dry procedure and bureaucratic tedium of inaccessible committee work, but should be educationally inspirational for the profession and the public, taking the agenda for change to governments.

Second, you can help create a new unionism that is imaginative not only behind the scenes in the many excellent staff development programmes that unions now run, but also in the forefront of its most public statements as well. Unions absolutely need members and leaders who will defend public education and teachers' working conditions against measures which will harm the quality of teaching and learning and deprofessionalize the teaching force. They also need leaders who can inspire their members, impel them to move forward, and impress the public in doing so. We need more change-oriented educators who develop their careers and their leadership through the unions. Are you such a person, or can you encourage others to run for office who are?

Third, if you have not already done so, join at least one professional body or network beyond your own school and become active in it, learning from and influencing other colleagues as you pursue professional learning and growth together.

Finally, invest in recreating the profession by working with student teachers and beginning teachers. When we discussed the future of teaching with teacher preparation students we were struck by the desire to make a difference coupled with the worry of becoming cynical and burnt out on the job. In the words of one student teacher, "as I was accepted into the programme, I went back to see some of my favourite teachers whom I thought would be supportive. Instead they were very pessimistic about the future. I want to make a difference but I hope I don't find my plans too idealistic and become burnt out." Faculties of education and their universities, in partnership with schools and districts, have a vital role to play here – something which they have not been good at in the past. (Fullan et al, 1998)

Make no mistake about it. Those entering teaching around the turn of the century – and new teachers will be entering in larger numbers for years to come – are entering at a time when transforming the profession is the main agenda. Guideline 6 anticipates that newcomers and experienced teachers will join forces to recreate the teaching profession. Getting "out there" means addressing the public perception that the profession of teaching does not monitor itself. It means engaging with external constituencies in establishing standards of performance. It means becoming a force for societal development. Recreating the profession is a collective quest. But it begins with you and thousands of colleagues like you making individual contributions of your own.

Guidelines for Principals

Principals are the gatekeepers and gate-openers of their schools. Connecting with what's "out there" in ways that really matter for students is almost impossible without their leadership, intervention and support. The following guidelines are written for principals, although they are also applicable to all leaders in the educational system including the many informal teacher leaders throughout our schools:

1. Steer clear of false certainty;

2. Base risk on security;

3. Respect those you want to silence;

4. Move towards the danger in forming new alliances;

5. Manage emotionally as well as rationally; *and*

6. Fight for lost causes (be hopeful when it counts).

1. STEER CLEAR OF FALSE CERTAINTY.

> *Singular recipes for success grabbed from leadership gurus, "bells and whistles workshops" or the latest management texts create dependency.*

In times of great uncertainty there is an understandable tendency to want to know what to do.

Stacey explains why:

> We respond to the fact that situations are uncertain and conflictual with a rigid injunction that people be more certain and more consensual. . . This denial of uncertainty itself allows us to sustain the fantasy of someone up there being in control and, perhaps, of things turning out for the best if we simply do what we are told, and so it protects us for a while from anxiety. However, because that defensive response involves dependency and a flight from reality, it hardly ever works.

(Stacey, 1996: 7-8)

Management, leadership and change gurus can bring about especially seductive kinds of dependency. Their charismatic authority promises people a way out of the chaos that they feel. Gurus cultivate dependent disciples rather than independent thinkers. In his study of the guru-phenomenon, psychiatrist Anthony Storr (1997: 233) says that this is because gurus need the reassurance and sense of certainty that having disciples gives them so they can cope with and put aside their own inner doubts. What disciples get out of the relationship is the comfort of someone else taking responsibility for their decisions. Storr eloquently warns us that "the charisma of certainty is a snare which entraps the child who is latent in us all." Disciples of modern gurus, he concludes, are "looking for what they want in the wrong place."

This is true of many educators and business leaders who have wasted precious time and resources looking for simple answers in the wrong places. Block (1993) proclaims:

> Write all the books you want. Give all the speeches you want. Run all the meetings you want. Bleat out your longing for how the world should work, and you will get only one question back. . . "How?" (p. 233)

There is no ready-made answer to the "how" question. Singular recipes for success grabbed from leadership gurus, "bells and whistles workshops" or the latest management texts create dependency. They oversimplify what it will take to bring about change in your own situation. Even when you know what research and published advice tells you, no one can prescribe exactly how to apply what you have learned ᵗᵒ your particular school and all the unique problems, opportunities and peculiarities it contains. Your own organization has its own special combination of personalities and prehistories. There is no one answer to the question of how one brings about change in specific situations. You can get ideas, directions, insights, and lines of thought, but you can never know exactly how to proceed. You have to beat the path by walking it.

Today's leaders must learn to think through solutions themselves (with assistance from their colleagues and communities). This is the essence of the learning organization. Management ideas and techniques are helpful, but only in the service of a critical mindset where educators draw deeply on their own local knowledge and insights.

Anxiety and self-doubt are understandable in a rapidly changing world, but management prescriptions and the proclamation of gurus which provide false certainty do us the disservice of closing down options and creating excessive dependency on charismatic individuals or abstract solutions. We need educational leaders who will push for change, but who also recognize that multiple options of connecting with what's "out there" must be explored and that new pathways must be 'beaten' as they do so. In the words of Saul (1995: 157), we need to "replace the race to certainty with a more relaxed approach to doubt."

2.   BASE RISK ON SECURITY.

In *What's Worth Fighting For?: Working Together For Your School*, we advised teachers and principals to develop a risk-taking mentality – to try new practices, get new learning and explore a wider range of solutions. This is all the more important "under a condition of uncertainty which is permanent and irreducible because of ceaseless social change" (Baumann, 1997: 21). Embracing risk and the uncertainty and messiness that accompanies it, is an important part of learning at the edge of chaos. Notwithstanding all the visceral emotion that may surround it, such risk-taking in conditions of great uncertainty can be an immense spur to creativity.

As Stacey argues:

> The creative process in human systems . . . is inevitably messy: it involves difference, conflict, fantasy, and emotion; it stirs up anger, envy, depression, and many other feelings. To remove the mess by inspiring us to follow some common vision, share the same culture, and pull together is to remove the mess that is the very raw material of creative activity.
>
> (Stacey, 1996: 15)

A certain level of anxiety is essential in making creative breakthroughs, although too much anxiety will also work against you. Heifetz (1994) talks about keeping "the level of distress within a tolerable range" when you are adapting to the demands of a difficult problem. Stacey (1996: 188) cautions that "to contain such anxiety, an individual requires a strong ego structure and a good enough 'holding environment,' which is to be found in the groups to which the individual belongs." What we need, argues Stacey, are "anxiety-containing" strategies that provide degrees of security within ourselves and in our relationships, without eliminating anxiety.

Here is the nub of an extremely important issue for administrators. The last thing we want is for legions of principals who are recent converts to chaos theory to go forward and gleefully throw their schools into disarray and to push the anxiety levels of their teachers and parents so high that no useful work gets done any more. Risk must be harmonized with security. As Baumann (1997: 3) puts it "freedom without security assures no more steady a supply of happiness than security without freedom."

The leadership challenge here can best be summarized in the diagram below:

	CERTAINTY	**UNCERTAINTY**
Security	*safety complacency*	*risk*
Insecurity	*fear hopelessness demoralization*	*frustration anxiety burnout*

The top left-hand cell describes teachers and schools who are "stuck" – not just anchored in tradition and routine, but trapped by it. Senses of personal security that come from supportive relationships and self validation, combined with a workplace where routines are predictable and certainty prevails, leave us with classrooms and teachers that are in a rut, impervious to change, not merely safe but complacent. In a rapidly changing world where the walls of the school are crumbling, this position is unsupportable and unsustainable. The principal's task here is to get teachers to question their complacency, and to move from a state of safety to one of risk.

The bottom right-hand cell describes an equally dangerous and dysfunctional extreme. Here, chaos is everywhere, risk turns to recklessness, and teachers pursue so many goals at once and with such intensity, that they lose all sense of focus. Over-eager teachers and their leaders can easily fall into this trap, pursuing one innovation after another and many all at once in desperate attempts to respond to successive outside initiatives in order to help their students. Schools like this suffer from projectitis – pursuing change frenetically through one uncompleted project after another. Teachers in these schools charge off in all directions. They experience their environment as completely unpredictable and have no time for the relationships that would give them enough sense of security and focus to set some priorities and operate from a stable base. As we saw in Oatley's (1992) work earlier, the result is an excess of negative and damaging emotion where pursuing too many goals at once, or failing to set priorities and complete goals, in circumstances where relationships and self-confidence are also weak, create frustration, anxiety and burnout. The principal's task here is to reduce risk, get some focus, and strengthen the culture of staff and community relationships.

The bottom left-hand cell describes many instances of all-encompassing, imposed change where the content and purpose of the change are repugnant to teachers and cannot be avoided by them – creating the certainty of despair. In addition, the breakneck speed of reform, along with instabilities introduced into working conditions and contracts destroy teachers' basic senses of ego, safety and security. The result is fear, despair, hopelessness and demoralization. Demoralization literally involves a loss of purpose or moral direction when you are forced to pursue other people's agendas, not your own. The results are transparent for all to see. In Australia, for example, where many of these conditions apply, only 4% of teachers report themselves as being "highly satisfied" with their work and only a total of 50% are satisfied at all. Typical of other jurisdictions undergoing top-down structural reforms, 59% of the 900 teachers in the sample say they are more dissatisfied now than they were earlier in their careers (Dinham & Scott, 1996).

Under circumstances of uncertainty and insecurity, the principal's task is to combat cultures of fear and hopelessness. Firstly, this can be achieved by developing strong collaborative cultures among the staff and with the community to build a sense of hope, security and strategy in which good things can be achieved educationally despite the conditions. A second way of combatting fear and hopelessness is by joining in and supporting the moral outrage, resistance and protest actions of teachers when governments go too far. Such strategies help teachers rebuild their sense of purpose, re-moralize their work, and resist or by-pass the morally questionable mandates of others.

In the top right-hand cell, risk is underpinned by security. The challenge for you as a principal in a context of increasing uncertainty is to give your teachers the security of being trusted and valued and of not being afraid to fail, so that they are keen and ready to experiment, to take risks, and to try new approaches. Value your settlers as well as your pioneers (but get them to talk to each other!). Learn together how to move forward from failure; don't go on a witch-hunt to find people to blame for it. Help develop a sense of collective purpose (re-moralize your school) that is ambitious but achievable, and that has reasonable coherence (neither too singular, nor all over the map). Don't let risk turn to recklessness. Provide security as well. Remember, positive emotions actually enhance rational decision-making because they help inform judgements in the face of imperfect knowledge and multiple goals.

3.   Respect Those You Want to Silence.

It is a mistake for principals to go only with like-minded innovators.

One reason why false certainty is dangerous is that it fails to take advantage of the intelligence of diversity. It alienates those who might disagree, making it unlikely that leaders "will either get things right" or get them implemented.

In *What's Worth Fighting For? Working Together For Your School,* we advised leaders in education to take a less stigmatizing and dismissive approach to teacher resistance to change. We urged more empathy with "resistant" teachers because their cautiousness about investing in change was often a rational response to bad changes or bad experiences with change in the past; or "resistance" might be due to health or other personal factors outside their work. But as well as being excusable, resistance to change can also be a powerful source of learning. Resisters may be right. They may have "good sense" in seeing through the change as faddish, misdirected and unworkable (Gitlin & Margonis, 1995). At the very least, their perspective on any change will be different and divergent from yours. Quell resistance and you remove the opportunities for learning. This applies to "resistant" teachers and parents alike.

'Resistance' to change can actually be highly instructive. Conflict can be exceedingly valuable in situations of diversity and complexity. Homogeneous cultures may have little disagreement but they are also much less interesting. Heterogeneous cultures risk greater conflict, but they also contain stronger seeds of breakthrough. As Maurer observes:

> *Often those who resist have something important to tell us. We can be influenced by them. People resist for what they view as good reasons. They may see alternatives we never dreamed of. They may understand problems about the minutiae of implementation that we never see from our lofty perch atop Mount Olympus.*
>
> (Maurer, 1996: 49)

According to Heifetz (1994), a counter-intuitive rule of thumb is required in order to reject "one's emotional impulse . . . to squash those in the community who raise disturbing questions. Consequently, an authority should protect those whom he [she] wants to silence. Annoyance is often a signal of opportunity" (p. 271).

It is a mistake for principals to go only with like-minded innovators. As Elmore (1995) puts it: "small groups of self-selected reformers apparently seldom influence their peers" (p. 20). They just create an even greater gap between themselves and others which eventually becomes impossible to bridge.

Beware of surrounding yourself only with innovative teachers and go-ahead parents who are pleasant to be with and reflect favourable images of yourself back to you. Not only does this insulate you from learning and different viewpoints elsewhere, but it also reduces the likelihood that your inner circle will disagree with you as well. They may be afraid of upsetting you or spoiling the special relationship you have together.

What can you do to learn from resistance or even join it, when it's valid? You can break staff and parents council meetings into smaller brainstorming groups sometimes so that opposing ideas are included without their advocates having to confront you directly. You can involve more skeptical colleagues and community groups in the earliest stages of innovation (learning from them and carrying their supporters with you as you go), instead of leaving them to be the last to know. When staff teams go to professional development meetings, invite a more "resistant" member to join them. Offer "resistant" colleagues and community members responsibilities. If they turn you down the first time, ask them again. Sometimes we have more to learn from our opponents and detractors, than we do from fellow travellers on the road of improvement. One of the key tasks of leadership is to create opportunities for learning from this kind of dissonance. To do that you have to respect and learn from differences.

4. MOVE TOWARDS THE DANGER IN FORMING NEW ALLIANCES.

Seeking external support, in fact, strengthens internal confidence and resiliency.

"Out there" beyond the school, today's environment may be dangerous but it is also laced with opportunities. In our previous books in the *What's Worth Fighting For* trilogy, we said that principals should foster and reinforce strong cultures of collaboration among teachers. It is now clear that schools cannot do this effectively unless they also incorporate external alliances. Seeking external support, in fact, strengthens internal confidence and resiliency. This is true of families and of other organizations as well (Skynner & Cleese, 1993). Indeed in their analysis of what distinguishes successful from unsuccessful reform efforts in hundreds of schools, Newmann & Wehlage (1995) found that external support was one of four key factors that made a difference. The boundaries of the collaborative culture must now be redrawn to include such wider communities of support.

These new relationships focus on transforming systems. While the transcendent power of hope can often lift particular individuals beyond the certainties and expectations of poverty and other disadvantages, it is not sufficient to help whole groups overcome the endemic conditions of failure. The origins of these problems are in society for which (we are often told) education can't compensate. Successful programmes, observes Schorr (1997: 6-7), see children in the context of their families, and deal with families as part of neighbourhoods and communities. What if society were to become a more active part of schooling rather than a place where schools simply deposit their graduates? Couldn't many schools and teachers, not just a few, begin to make a difference then? Moving towards the danger means establishing new partnerships in which entire *systems* are the focus of change: schools, families, neighbourhoods and cities in concert.

New relationships are also about gaining allies. When dubious reform agendas throw schools into turmoil, and teachers and schools are discredited as failing by government advertising and media reports, solid public support can make a world of difference to teachers. If it is strong enough, this support can even combat policy itself. Moving towards the danger in the environment is essential to capture the public's imagination about teaching and to garner its support for those times when education and teachers come under attack.

If we are to reframe the relationship with the outside as we move towards it, the principal's role will be pivotal. Not every prospective partner is panting for involvement in the school. This is new terrain not only for principals and teachers but for external partners as well. Some parents are ambivalent or reticent about involvement. Others are aggressive and intrusive. Business leaders do not always know how best to engage the school other than by supplying resources, making unhelpful judgements, or treating schools as mere markets. Principals must lead the way in guiding people through this new terrain.

Scanning the horizon is a key strategy. In Chapter 3, we presented evidence that most principals and other administrators don't do this very well. They have no coordinated way of responding to changes in the external environment. Schools may develop missions and visions of where they want to go, but these are preferred futures built on ideals and dreams. What administrators, teachers and communities also need to do is sketch out and consider other scenarios, positive and negative, with which they may need to engage in the near future, so they will not be caught off-guard by new developments (Schwartz, 1991).

First, principals must build strong relationships with parents and the community. They must make school councils into capacity-building entities for mobilizing parents and the community, instead of stagnant structures. The multiple ways in which connections can be made with parents must be examined critically and carefully. It is important to make it as easy for teachers to question the desirability and feasibility of new forms of community involvement as it is to get them on board. In all this, good relationships, nurtured carefully and developed patiently, through innumerable conversations and interactions, are essential.

As an unemployed male parent said in a project we are undertaking in four U.S. school districts with the Rockefeller Foundation, "we parents have to figure out how to relate to teachers in a way that is not threatening to them." Once you move towards the danger of your communities, you will find that parents have immense reserves of empathy and support to draw on and contribute.

Moving towards the danger is equally important in relation to government policy, especially in terms of assessment and accountability issues. The point is not to dedicate all one's energies to discrediting official information or vetoing its relevance, but to take charge of your own assessment and accountability procedures – carefully examining externally gathered student performance data, collecting your own information, portraying your own school, and leading the debate about planning for improvement. If principals take their school's accountability to the public, they will be more credible (and better supported) when they contest the methods by which governments hold them accountable in turn. Investing in professional development to help teachers become more assessment-literate is a vital part of this quest. Assigning positions of responsibility to teachers who will take charge of assessment, research and accountability issues can also be useful.

Technology presents similar opportunities and dangers. Basic technological literacy is the most minimal objective for introducing computers and other machines into classrooms. The deeper benefits accrue when educators become experts in using and designing technology to transform the nature and quality of student learning. Implementors of new technology too often talk about hardware, software, programmes and machines, but not about how all this might fundamentally change and improve teaching and learning. The real revolution in technology will turn out to be not the speed and sophistication of computers, but how teachers use technological developments to push back the frontiers of learning in terms of how to think and to apply knowledge.

The same difficult balancing act is involved in moving towards the danger of corporate connections. Growing numbers of businesses are developing explicit philosophies and programmes directed at the common good, through philanthropic donations, social development projects, and school-work programs that can benefit the school and the business alike. Other business involvements are more questionable. Educators must neither embrace nor dismiss all possible business partnerships – but develop a philosophy and a code of responsible marketing which will guide them in selecting the kinds of partnerships they want. Similarly, principals must reach into business people's hearts and not just their pockets – finding out, connecting with and nurturing what each potential business partner cares about educationally as a parent, a citizen or a former student, and not just as someone with access to a large bank account.

The principal's role then is to help establish reciprocity with the outside. This includes, as we said earlier in this chapter, a more proactive relationship with the media. Be open about problems, use your school's successes as a source of confidence, and never lose sight of the fact that you and your colleagues are doing important work.

In short, just as the principal of the last decade (1987-1997) was urged to develop collaborative cultures within schools, the principal of the next decade (1998-2008) should be leading the way to redefine collaboration so that it encompasses alliances with groups and individuals outside the school.

5.   MANAGE EMOTIONALLY AS WELL AS RATIONALLY.

If you are a leader, someone will always be dissatisfied with your performance.

As a leader, and as you move with your staff towards many external dangers in a world of diversity and uncertainty, you cannot invite disagreement and dissonance without attending to your own and others' emotional health.

As Maurer (1996: 59) says, "dealing with resistance can be very stressful. People attack you and your precious ideas. Sometimes they seem to show no respect for you." If you are a leader, someone will always be dissatisfied with your performance. The wider the world you connect with, the more dissatisfaction you will get (although you will also get more support as well). Relaxation is vital here. The more you relax, the easier it will be to acknowledge and embrace the resistance of others. Maurer suggests a number of methods for relaxing including: physical exercise, relaxation exercises, recalling a higher purpose, teaming up with a supportive partner, separating self from role, laughter and (not least) ignoring the temptation to get even (p. 164-167). Doing these things is an important part of developing your own emotional intelligence as a leader.

As well as relaxing, the emotionally intelligent leader also seeks help and emotional support from others. In their comparison of healthy families and organizations, Skynner and Cleese (1993) observe that:

> *The healthy families will be clear about their emotional needs so they won't have any hesitation about stopping to take a rest if they need to, or asking for help or advice when they want that. But it's the last of these factors, the degree of emotional support that they can draw on, which mainly accounts for the ease with which they deal with change (p. 32).*

The three kinds of support that Skynner and Cleese say contributed to personal and collective resilience in the face of change, should now be familiar: good relationships, connections in the community, and a transcendent value system, i.e., the purpose and passion of "going beyond just the welfare of themselves, or even of their family" (p. 33).

So how can you manage emotionally as well as rationally? Here are just a few pointers. Ask people directly how they feel – especially during a difficult meeting that seems to be 'stuck'. Show how you *feel* (not to excess, of course) and express your authenticity as a leader. Ask for help not just when you are delegating busywork (and therefore completely in control), but when you genuinely do not know what to do. Show empathy for other people's viewpoints and what gives rise to them, even though you may disagree.

Make parents feel secure and wanted, however angry or difficult they may be. Try and break down at least some meetings and professional development time into smaller groups so that people can get emotionally and intellectually engaged. Talk to people and spend time with them.

In schools which engage more and more with the external environment and where change is ever-present, the role of the leader is also to help teachers, parents and others develop strategies that contain anxiety. Providing a basic sense of security is essential here (Guideline 2), through building relationships that emphasize trust, compassion, empathy, laughter and care. In tandem with this emotional support and release, it is also important to lead your staff and community in honest self-reflection about the work of the school and your own efforts in it, to articulate issues clearly and pose insightful questions about them, and to help others think their way through the complex matters before them.

Managing emotionally means putting high priority on *reculturing* your school and its relationship to what's "out there", and not merely *restructuring* it. Restructuring refers to changes in the formal structure of schooling in terms of organization, timetables, roles and the like. It has a terrible track record. Incessant restructuring in education as a sole strategy of reform bears no relationship to improving teaching and learning. Lengthening the school year, changing funding formulae, or realigning roles at the school level do little by themselves to bring about improvement.

Reculturing by contrast, involves changing the norms, values, incentives, skills and relationships in an organization to support (and prod) people to work differently together. The goal is to create more collaborative work cultures. Reculturing *does* make a difference in teaching and learning. The cumulative evidence is that students learn much better when principals, teachers and others develop a professional learning community among themselves, focus on improving teaching and learning, examine and act on assessment data in relation to what students are learning, and connect with external communities and resources to support them in their efforts (Newmann & Wehlage, 1995).

Reculturing requires strong emotional investment from principals and everyone else connected with a school. Structural change is part of the picture of successful reform so that the timetable allows all students (and not just a few) to get work experience, so that parents' nights change for the better, or so that computers become an integral part of every classroom, for example. But structural change only works after people have invested emotionally in transforming the culture and relationships in a school over many years. When schools have been recultured, teachers and community members together start to push for changes in the structure because they see how such changes will benefit their students. Structures are only as good as the relationships and know-how of the people who occupy them. Emotional management is ultimately about attending to these relationships properly. Managing emotionally and rationally in today's turbulent times *is* rocket science. It calls for sophisticated leaders who are good at fighting for the right things in the right way.

6.   FIGHT FOR LOST CAUSES.

Principals with hope are much less likely to succumb to the daily stresses of the job.

In *Mr. Smith Goes to Washington*, a Frank Capra movie from the 1930s, James Stewart plays a young man just elected to the Senate. He receives some seemingly absurd advice from his father – "Lost causes are the only things worth fighting for!" A significant step toward liberation for principals and for teachers is to realize that a hopeful stance in the face of seemingly intractable problems is the most healthy, constructive thing they can do. As we have seen, this does not mean that principals should pretend that everything is rosy. Leaders who display 'unwarranted optimism' go after difficult problems with fervour.

Fighting for lost causes may mean not giving up on difficult students whom everyone else has abandoned. Or it may mean not giving in to governments whose reforms don't have students' interests at heart. The scale of the struggle may vary, but the principle is the same.

Fighting for lost causes brings us back to hope. As Vaclav Havel, President of the Czech Republic and no stranger to fighting for lost causes, observes:

> *Hope is definitely not the same thing as optimism. It is not the conviction that something will turn out well, but the certainty that something makes sense, regardless of how it turns out. It is hope, above all, that gives us strength to live and to continually try new things, even in conditions that seem hopeless.*
>
> (Havel, 1993:68)

Principals with hope are much less likely to succumb to the daily stresses of the job. They place their problems in a loftier perspective that enables them to rebound from bad days. Once leaders realize that having hope is not a prediction, that it is independent of knowing how things might turn out, it becomes a deeper resource. Leaders with hope are less likely to panic when faced with immediate and pressing problems.

It is especially important that leaders have and display hope, that they show they are prepared to fight for lost causes, because they set the tone for so many others. Teachers with purpose are desperate for life-lines of hope. They understand that hope is not a promise, but they need to be reminded that they are connected to a larger purpose, and to others who are struggling to make progress as well. Articulating and discussing hope when the going gets rough re-energizes teachers, reduces stress, and can point to new directions. In teaching, resilience is an essential capacity and hope is its regenerative fuel. It can be found in a class of difficult students, in a staffroom of committed colleagues, or in protests of defiance against educational policies that threaten the common good.

Principals will be much more effective (and healthier) if they develop and pursue high hopes as they reculture their schools and their relationships to the outside.

Guidelines for Governments

The main purpose of the trilogy is to provide ideas and action guidelines for teachers and principals. How ironic that the typical reform strategies used by governments so alienate and thereby grossly underutilize those very people who are most central to successful reform. If governments are really interested in substantial improvement for all students, they must engage with the evidence regarding reform strategies which really do deepen and make a difference to student learning and avoid self-defeating strategies which, despite repeated use, have had virtually no positive effects at all in the past. Government leaders who recognize the power of capacity-building strategies, along with frameworks of accountability, will achieve significantly more change 'on the ground' than those that employ distant hierarchical methods of compliance.

Micklethwait and Wooldridge (1996: 294), remind us of two problems that plague public policy-making.

> *The first is that the state is an incredibly blunt instrument; it gets hold of one overarching idea and imposes it without any sensitivity to the local context. The second is the desperate craving of politicians for a magical solution.*

Our advice to governments comes in the form of five brief, but deeply powerful guidelines.

1.   INVEST IN THE LONG TERM.

In her impressive review of large scale social programmes, Schorr (1997) found that "successful programs have a long-term, preventive orientation, a clear mission, and continue to evolve over time." As hard as it is for politicians to do, if they are serious about reform, they must base their strategies on approaches that have the best record of success educationally, not what is easy or popular politically. This means investing in the right long-term solutions that will make a difference, but that may not come to fruition before the next election. We have shown that early childhood education is one of the best investments there is, but its benefits are seen long after governments who introduce it have gone out of office. Most change strategies that make a difference in the classroom take five years or more to yield results – again, out of phase with most political election cycles. Governments must put educational investment beyond their own needs for political survival. By showing such integrity they may paradoxically gain greater political support.

2. GO BEYOND LEFT AND RIGHT.

Neither idealize conventional state bureaucracies of the past, nor over-zealously embrace the idea of more market-like systems of school choice (with all their divisive consequences). Beyond the ideologies of left and right, the real issues are how can local level bureaucracies be agencies of support rather than interference and control for schools and parents? How can parents be offered choice within parameters that protect equity and diversity? How can school systems and collective agreements be made more flexible so schools can open up to and get more help from their communities without exploiting teachers or creating excessive insecurity for them? These are the real rather than rhetorical challenges of school system reorganization.

3. USE DATA FOR IMPROVEMENT, NOT EMBARRASSMENT.

Ensure that assessment and accountability measures aren't used gratuitously or exploitatively to shame public education and create government pretexts for reorganizing it. How can data be contextualized fairly to present schools' performance in relation to the communities they serve? How can we hold schools accountable for how they improve over time (i.e., value-added measures of achievement) more than how they compare with schools in other very different communities? How can data be used as a spur to greater success rather than as a way to justify government's obsession with educational failure (which they then have an excuse to fix)?

4. PUT CAPACITY-BUILDING BEFORE COMPLIANCE.

Don't humiliate teachers for their alleged failures, or bluntly demand they do better – but actually invest time and resources in professional development and opportunities for collaboration (within a clearly defined framework of standards that teachers have helped develop themselves), so that teachers are provided with the means to improve over time. Capacity-building means helping teachers and communities to be able to respond effectively to changes that come their way and to improve continuously as a lifelong obligation so that standards will keep rising all the time. Compliance is about putting out fires (sometimes ones that governments have lit themselves). Capacity-building is about preventing fires occurring in the first place. No complex social reform has ever worked without investing in local capacity-building. If you want to spread and sustain good ideas, you have to spread the conditions that make good ideas effective, not just the ideas alone. These conditions pertain to local context, local relationships and local capacity.

5. DEAL WITH THE DEMOGRAPHICS.

> *You cannot attract high calibre people to a profession which has been subjected to unabated denigration and demoralization.*

Look at the age profile of the teaching force where, almost everywhere, huge cohorts of teachers are heading for retirement in the coming years and a massive renewal of the teaching force will be needed. You cannot attract high calibre people to a profession which has been subjected to unabated denigration and demoralization. Aside from early childhood development, the next best investment that governments can make is to use the next decade to help redefine and reinvigorate the teaching profession. Few policy initiatives will have greater long-term payoff than redesigning teacher education from the beginning to the end of the career (along with reculturing schools and their communities).

Guidelines for Parents

New relationships between parents and schools are a two-way street. Although we have said that schools do not capitalize enough on the interest in and knowledge of their own children's learning that many parents have, it is it is also true that many parents are insufficiently involved in the education of their children. While schools have often not made parental involvement easy or have otherwise resisted it, many parents may need to act differently as well. For parents, we would advise.

1. PRESS GOVERNMENTS TO CREATE THE KIND OF TEACHERS YOU WANT.

Help make education a sophisticated election issue that goes beyond hackneyed slogans to address how we can make teaching better so that learning will get better too. Demand answers regarding the kinds of resources that will be dedicated to that end. How we will get and keep quality teachers? How will teachers be helped and encouraged to maintain and improve that quality over time? Better learning needs better teaching – how, precisely, will governments bring that about? Push them for answers.

2. LEAVE NOSTALGIA BEHIND YOU.

What worked in 1965 is unlikely to be suitable for 1995 or 2005.

Make more efforts to understand what schools are striving to achieve in today's world. Try and get first-hand knowledge and experience of what your children's school is doing now. Consider the knowledge and skills your children will need as they become citizens and workers in the future, and what kinds of teaching and learning are necessary to create these. Don't long for your children to have exactly the kind of education you think you remember having yourself, just because that is what's familiar to you. The science of learning is profoundly different today. Find out more about these new developments. What worked in 1965 is unlikely to be suitable for 1995 or 2005 (Stoll and Fink, 1996). Remember the words of Christopher Lasch (1991) – that "nostalgia is the abdication of memory."

3. ASK WHAT YOU CAN DO FOR YOUR SCHOOL AS WELL AS WHAT YOUR SCHOOL CAN DO FOR YOU.

What can you offer and contribute to support your school? The best place to start is at home. If you expect the school to develop a work ethic in your child, do you also insist on this at home by making sure he or she really does mow the lawns, shovel the snow, complete his or her homework, etc. The more you give to your school and its teachers, the more responsiveness you are likely to get when you want something in return. Once more, relationships are the key.

4.   PUT PRAISE BEFORE BLAME.

If you have criticisms to make of your children's education, remember that the teachers will be as anxious about meeting you as you are about meeting them. Try to put teachers at their ease. Put compliments before criticism. Wherever you can, see what the school is doing first-hand, so you know your complaints aren't groundless. Contact teachers and thank them spontaneously when things are going well (which will make the more difficult encounters easier and put them into perspective). Take responsibility to build relationships with your children's teachers *before* problems arise.

Life-lines of Hope

> *Above all, as general polls confirm, education has become the number one policy priority in the minds of citizens in many countries.*

We have talked a lot about hope in this book, and also about creating the conditions in which hopefulness can bloom. In the depths of despair where many teachers and parents have come to find themselves, we believe we are on the edge of some of the most hopeful times in education we have seen for decades. As we write, the first signs of this turnaround are already evident in some parts of the world. Major commitments have been made in California and England to reduce class sizes and infuse more teachers into early childhood and primary education. The United States has produced a visionary report on "The Future of Teaching" and a national Senate Commission is sitting in Australia on "The Status of Teaching". Meanwhile, in England, policy advisors to a new Labour Government are puzzling through ways to reinvigorate teaching with stronger support and better professional development. This is not yet a revolution; but it is an important start.

These changes of heart in educational policy are attuned not only to crises of recruitment in the profession but also to important shifts in the public mood. The baby boomers are leaving the egocentric eighties behind them when economic survival, taking care of their own families, getting-on and sometimes outright greed dominated personal and policy agendas. As the baby boomers age and their children leave home, their lives are taking on different preoccupations. Foot shows what the demographic signs auger in *Boom, Bust and Echo* (1996: 126-127) when he observes that volunteering will grow in the years to come as populations age and people have more time to devote to worthy causes. The pollster, Angus Reid (1996: 218), predicts that "over the next few decades, an emphasis on emotional growth will overtake the post-war preoccupation with material well-being."

People are increasingly searching for what connects them to others in the community now, rather than striving for individual advancement at any price. With community and compassion coming in from the sidelines, governments which focus on naming and shaming public education for its failures, on cutting deeper and deeper into systems of educational support, and on attacking the integrity and professionalism of teachers will find the public less and less receptive to their efforts. Although hope for many teachers may now seem at its lowest ebb, the tide for reinventing and reinvesting in public education is already starting to turn.

Above all, as general polls confirm, education has become the number one policy priority in the minds of citizens in many countries. People know that now more than ever a healthy education system is vital for the life chances of their children and grandchildren. Indeed, they know that it is vital for societal survival and the public good in their local community and the world at large. People place education as their top priority, not just because they know that it is crucial, but also because they are profoundly worried that current reform strategies are not working.

In education, then, we have a significant priority with a gravely precarious future. The possibilities of acting for the common good are enormous. But the dangers are equally great. It will not take much for the educational edifice to fall into complete disarray. Creating, pursuing and being guided by life-lines of hope can help all of us mobilize the forces to claim education as a societal priority of utmost importance.

We have not provided a 'how to' book. Prescriptions are an invitation to dependency. Our own invitation is to move towards a new consciousness, and new relationships which have been seriously neglected until now. Never has there been a more critical time to get out there and confront differences and work through the discomfort of diversity in order to achieve new breakthroughs for all the students we teach. The positive potential of taking this risk is far preferable to minding our own business in our classrooms and homes, and doing nothing at all.

In getting "out there", follow Kingsolver's (1997) advice in *Animal Dreams:*

> *The very least you can do in your life is to figure out what you hope for.*
> *And the most you can do is live inside that hope. Not admire it from*
> *a distance but live right in it, under its roof. (p. 299)*

It is not only up to teachers and administrators to figure out and work for what they hope for: it is up to parents, students, policymakers, labour and business leaders, politicians, and the media as well. Rebuilding and redefining education, and its relationship to the world "out there", in other words, is a job for citizens and for society as a whole. *What's Worth Fighting Out There?* is ultimately about developing life-lines of hope with all those teachers, students, and communities who are desperately seeking a way forward.

REFERENCES

Ashton, P. & Webb, R. (1986). *Making a difference: Teacher's sense of efficacy.* New York: Longman.

Barlow, M. & Robertson, H. J. (1994). *Class warfare: The assault on Canada's schools.* Toronto: Key Porter Books.

Bauman, Z. (1997). *Postmodernity and its discontents.* Cambridge: Polity Press.

Beresford, E. (1992). The politics of parental involvement. In G. Allen and Martin (Eds.), *Education and Community: The politics of practice.* London: Cassell, 44-55.

Berliner, D. & Biddle, B. (1995). *The manufactured crisis.* Reading, MA: Addison Wesley

Bigum, C. & Kenway, J. (in press). New information technologies and the ambiguous future of schooling. In A. Hargreaves, A. Lieberman, M. Fullan, & D. Hopkins (Eds.), *International handbook of educational change.* Dordrecht, The Netherlands: Kluwer Press.

Binney, G. & Williams, C. (1995). *Leaning into the future.* London: Nicholas Brealey.

Bishop, P. & Mulford, W. (1996). Empowerment in four Australian primary schools. *International Journal of Educational Reform, 5*(2), 193-204.

Blase, J. & Anderson, G. (1995). *The micropolitics of educational leadership.* London: Cassell.

Block, P. (1987). *The empowered manager.* San Francisco, CA: Jossey-Bass.

Block, P. (1993). *Stewardship.* San Francisco, CA: Berrett Koehler.

Bridges, W. (1994). *Jobshift.* Reading, MA: Addison-Wesley.

Budge, D. (1997). "One in three wants to quit." *Times Educational Supplement,* January.

Campbell, E. (1996). Ethical implications of collegial loyalty as one view of teacher professionalism. *Teachers and teaching: Theory and Practice, 2*(2), 191-208.

Coleman, J. (1990). *Foundations of social theory.* Cambridge, MA: Harvard University Press.

Cszikzentmihaly, M. (1990). *Flow: The psychology of optimal experience.* New York: Harper & Collins.

Cszikzentmihaly, M. (1996). *Creativity: Flow and the psychology of discovery and invention.* New York: Harper Collins.

Cummins, J. (in press). Language issues and educational change. In A. Hargreaves, A. Lieberman, M. Fullan, & D. Hopkins (Eds.), *International handbook of educational change.* Dordrecht, The Netherlands: Kluwer Press.

Damasio, A. (1994). *Descartes error.* New York: Grosset Putnam.

Darling-Hammond, L. (1992). Reframing the school reform agenda. *The School Administrator*, November, 22-27.

de Gues, A. (1997). *The living company.* Cambridge, MA: Harvard Business School Press.

Delpit, L. (1993). *Other people's children: Cultural conflict in the classroom.* New York: The New Press.

Dinham, S. and Scott, C (1996). *The teacher 2000 project: A study of teacher motivation and health.* Penrith: University of Western Sydney, Nepean.

Dolan, P. (1994). *Restructuring our schools.* Kansas City, MO: Systems and Organizations.

Dryden, K. (1995). *In school.* Toronto: McClelland Publications.

Earl, L. & LeMahieu, P. (1997). Rethinking assessment and accountability. In A. Hargreaves (Ed.), *Rethinking educational change with heart and mind* (pp. 149-168). The 1997 ASCD Yearbook. Alexandria, VA: The Association for Supervision and Curriculum Development.

Elkind, D. (1997). Schooling in the postmodern world. In A. Hargreaves (Ed.), *Rethinking educational change with heart and mind* (pp. 27-42). Alexandria, VA: Association for Supervision and Curriculum Development.

Elmore, R. (1995). *Getting to scale with good educational practice.* Harvard Educational Review, 66(1), 1-26.

Epstein, J. (1995). School/family/community partnerships. *Phi Delta Kappan, 76,* 701-712.

Etzioni, A. (1993). *The spirit of community.* New York: Croan Publishers.

Evans, R. (1996). *The human side of school change.* San Francisco: Jossey-Bass.

Farson, R. (1996). *Management of the absurd.* New York: Simon & Schuster.

Foot, D. with Stoffman, D. (1996). *Boom, bust and echo: How to profit from the coming demographic shift.* Toronto: MacFarlane, Walter and Ross.

Franklin, U. (1997, September 8). Opening address of the Canadian Educational Association National Convention on Creating school success.

Freire, P. (1982). *Pedagogy of the oppressed.* Harmondsworth: Penguin.

Fried, R. (1995). *The passionate teacher.* Boston: Beacon Press.

Fullan, M. (1993). *Change forces: Probing the depths of educational reform.* London: Falmer Press.

Fullan, M. (1997). Emotion and hope: Constructive concepts for complex times. In A. Hargreaves (Ed.), *Rethinking educational change with heart and mind* (pp. 216-233). Alexandria, VA: Association for Supervision and Curriculum Development.

Fullan, M. (1997). *What's worth fighting for in the principalship?* (2nd ed.). Toronto: Ontario Public School Teachers' Federation; New York: Teachers College Press.

Fullan, M. & Hargreaves, A. (1992). *What's worth fighting for? Working together for your school.* Toronto: Ontario Public School Teachers' Federation; New York: Teachers College Press.

Fullan, M., Galuzzo, G., Morris, P. & Watson, N. (1998). *The rise and stall of teacher education reform.* Washington, DC: American Association of Colleges of Teacher Education.

Fullan, M. & Watson, N. with Kilcher, A. (1997). *Building infrastructures for professional development*. New York: The Rockefeller Foundation.

Galbraith, J. (1992). *The culture of contentment*. Boston: Houghton Mifflin Co.

Galbraith, J. (1996). *The good society*. Boston: Houghton Mifflin Co.

Gates, W. (1995). *The road ahead*. New York: Viking Press.

Gardner, H. (1991). *The unschooled mind*. New York: Basic Books.

Gitlin, A. & Margonis, F. (1995). The political aspect of reform. *The American Journal of Education, 103*, 377-405.

Goleman, D. (1995). *Emotional intelligence*. New York: Bantam Books.

Goodlad, J. (1994). *Educational renewal: Better teachers, better schools*. San Francisco: Jossey-Bass.

Goodlad, J. (1997). *In praise of education*. New York: Teachers College Press.

Handy, C. (1994). *The age of paradox*. Cambridge, MA: Harvard Business Press.

Hargreaves, A. (1994). *Changing teachers, changing times: Teachers' work and culture in the postmodern age*. London: Cassell; New York: Teachers College Press; Toronto: University of Toronto Press.

Hargreaves, A. & Earl, L. with Manning, S. and Moore, S. (1997). *Learning to change: A study of teachers committed to innovation in grades 7 & 8* (Final project report). Toronto: Ontario Institute for Studies in Education at the University of Toronto.

Hargreaves, A., Earl, L. & Ryan, J. (1996). *Schooling for change*. New York: Falmer Press.

Hargreaves, D. (1982). *The challenge for the comprehensive school*. London: Routledge and Kegan Paul.

Helsby, G. & Knight, P. (1997). Continuing professional development and the National Curriculum. In G. Helsby & G. McCulloch (Eds.), *Teachers and the National Curriculum*. London: Cassell, 145-162.

Havel, V. (1993, October). Never hope against hope. *Esquire*, 65-69.

Heifetz, R. (1994). *Leadership without easy answers.* Cambridge, MA: Harvard University Press.

Henry, M. (1996). *Parent-school collaboration.* Albany: State University of New York Press.

Hochschild, A. (1997) *The Time Bind.* New York: Metropolitan Books.

Jeffrey, B. & Woods, P. (1997). Feeling deprofessionalized. *The Cambridge Journal of Education,* 325-343.

Kanter, R.M. (1996). World-class leaders: the power of partnering. In Hesselbein, F., Goldsmith, M. & Beckhand, R., (Eds.), *The leader of the future* (pp. 89-98). New York: The Drucker Foundation.

Keating, D. (1996). Habits of the mind for a learning society: Educating for human development. In Olson, D., & Torrance, N., (Eds.), *Handbook of education and human development* (pp. 461-481). Oxford: Blackwell.

Kenway, J., Bigum, C., Fitzclarence, L. and Collier, J. (1995) Educationally and socially responsible marketing. Keynote address, Australian Capital Territory Principals' Association Conference, March, 1995.

Kingsolver, B. (1990). *Animal dreams.* New York: Harper Collins.

Koestler, A. (1967). *The ghost in the machine.* London: Hutchinson.

Labaree, D. (1997). *How to succeed in school without really learning: The credentials race in American education.* New Haven and London: Yale University Press.

Lasch, C. (1991). *The true and only heaven: Progress and its critics.* New York: W. W. Norton.

Levin, B. & Riffel, J. A. (1997). *Schools and the changing world.* London: Falmer Press.

Lieberman, A. & Grolnick, M. (1997). Networks, reform and the professional development of teachers. In A. Hargreaves, (Ed.) *Rethinking educational change with heart and mind,* The 1997 ASCD Yearbook: Alexandria, VA: the Association for Supervision and Curriculum Development, 192-215.

Lucas Educational Foundation. (1997). *Learn and Live*. San Rafael, CA: Author.

Manitoba School Improvement Program (1997). Toronto and Winnipeg: Walter and Duncan Gordon Charitable Foundation.

Maurer, R. (1996). *Beyond the wall of resistance*. Austin, TX: Bard Books.

Meier, D. (1987). Central Park East: An alternative story. *Phi Delta Kappan, 68*(10), 753-757.

Mertz, C. & Furman, G. (1997). *Community and schools: Promise and paradox*. New York: Teachers College Press.

Metz, M. (1991) *Real School: a universal drama amid disparate experience*. In D. Michael and M. Gresta (Eds) Education politics for the new century, the twentieth anniversary yearbook of the Politics of Education Association. London: Falmer Press, 75-92.

Micklethwait, J., & Wooldridge, A. (1996). *The witch doctors: Making sense of management gurus*. New York: Times Books, Random House.

Mintzberg, H. (1994). *The rise and fall of strategic planning*. New York: Free Press.

National Commission on the Future of Teaching in America (1996). *What matters most: Teaching for America's future*. Washington, DC: Author.

Newmann, F., & Wehlage, G. (1995). *Successful school restructuring*. Madison, WI: Center on Organization and Restructuring of Schools.

Nodding, N. (1992). *The challenge to care in schools*. New York: Teachers College Press.

Oatley, K. (1992). *Best laid schemes: The psychology of emotions*. Cambridge: Cambridge University Press.

Oatley, K., & Jenkins, J. (1996). *Understanding emotions*. Cambridge, MA: Blackwell.

Ontario Royal Commission on Learning (1994). *For the love of learning, I-V*. Toronto, ON: Queen's Printer.

Organization for Economic Cooperation and Development (1994). *The jobs study.* Paris, France: Author.

Organization for Economic Cooperation and Development (1997). *Failure at school: Problems and policies.* Paris, France: Author.

Postman, N. (1992). *Technopoly.* New York: Alfred A. Knopf.

Putnam, R. (1993). *Making democracy work.* Princeton, NJ: Princeton University Press.

Reid, A. (1996). *Shakedown: How the new economy is changing our lives.* Toronto: Doubleday.

Rudduck, J., Chaplain, R., & Wallace, G. (1996). *School improvement: What can pupils tell us.* London: David Fulton.

Rudduck, J., Day, J., & Wallace, G. (1997). Students perspectives on school improvement. In A. Hargreaves (Ed.), *Rethinking educational change with heart and mind,* The ASCD Yearbook. Alexandria, VA: The Association for Supervision and Curriculum Development, 73-91.

Rury, J., & Mirel, J. (1997). The political economy of urban education. *Review of Education, 22,* 49-112.

Saul, J. (1995). *The unconscious civilization.* Toronto: Anansi Press.

Sarason, S. (1982). *The culture of the school and the problem of change* (2nd ed.). Boston: Allyn & Bacon.

Sarason, S. (1995). *Parent involvement and the political principle.* San Francisco, CA: Jossey-Bass.

Sarason, S. (1990). *The predictable failure of educational reform.* San Francisco: Jossey-Bass.

Scardamalia, M. (1997). Sociocognitive design issues for interactive learning environments across knowledge building communities. Paper presented at the annual meeting of the American Educational Research Association.

Scardamalia, M. & Bereiter, C. (1996). Engaging students in a knowledge society. *Educational Leadership, 54* (3), 6-10.

Schorr, L. (1997). *Common purpose: Strengthening families and neighborhoods to rebuild America.* New York: Doubleday, Anchor Books.

Schrage, M. (1990). *Shared minds.* New York: Random House.

Schwartz, P. (1991). *The art of the long view.* New York: Doubleday.

Sergiovanni, T. (1992). *Moral leadership: Getting to the heart of school improvement.* San Francisco: Jossey-Bass.

Shimahara, K. & Sakai, A. (1995). *Learning to teach in two cultures: Japan and the United States.* New York: Galard Publishers.

Sikes, P. (1997). *Parents who teach.* London: Cassell.

Sizer, T. (1992). *Horace's school.* Boston: Houghton Mifflin.

Skynner, R., & Cleese, J. (1993). *Life and how to survive it.* London: Methuen.

Stacey, R. (1996). *Complexity and creativity in organizations.* San Francisco, CA: Berrett-Koehler.

Steinberg, L. (1996). *Beyond the classroom: Why school reform has failed and what parents need to do.* New York: Simon & Schuster.

Stoll, C. (1995). *Silicon snake oil.* New York: Doubleday.

Stoll, L. & Fink, D. (1996). *Changing our schools.* Buckingham: Open University Press.

Storr, A. (1997). *Feet of clay: A study of gurus.* London: Harper Collins.

Times Education Supplement (1997). *Times Education Supplement Survey.* London: Author.

Vincent, C. (1996). *Parents and teachers.* London; Bristol, PA: Falmer Press.

Walsh, J. 1997). *Stories of renewal: Community building and the future of urban America.* New York: The Rockefeller Foundation.

Werner, E., & Smith, R. (1992). *Overcoming the odds.* Ithaca, NY: Cornell University Press.

Wynn, J. (1994). Continuing inequalities into new times. In J. Wynn (Ed.). *Schooling, what future? Balancing an education agenda.* Deakin, Australia: Deakin Centre for Education and Change, 101-111.